Praise

'Beware. This looks like it should be a book for property managers. The reality is this is a book for council chief executives, finance directors and any and every councillor anywhere near a council's cabinet. It asks you to think. It asks you to question. It will amuse and terrify, often on the same page.

It reminds all that we hold property for a purpose, and that property is about people as much as being an asset, and that we often fail to think about property in the round.'
— **Keith House,** Leader of Eastleigh Borough Council

'*The Property Strategy Handbook* is an insightful, pragmatic and easy-to-follow guide, grounded with experience and punctuated with tips and case studies. This is a must read.'
— **Stuart Timmiss,** Executive Director of Place, Economy & Environment, West Northamptonshire Council

'As ever, we get taken on a rollercoaster journey with Chris Brain. With the help of Jodie Foster, Sherlock Holmes and Buddha I certainly felt that I managed to reach my personal lightbulb moment...!'
— **Geoff Bacon,** Head of Property Services, Swansea Council

'It is so difficult to express how good this book is. It is hard to find the words to do it justice. They struggle to convey my genuine enjoyment from reading it. This is a map out of the asset management wilderness, in a practical pocket-sized guide. Truly empowering.'
— **Abi Marshall,** Property Commissioning Manager, Gloucester City Council

'The book provides confidence that what matters is not the plan, but the planning, with clear focus on changing the mindset across a spectrum of differing stakeholders. The book provides decades of thought, experience and case studies.'
— **Paul Jones,** Executive Director of Finance, Assets and Regeneration, Cheltenham Borough Council

'This book will leave you thinking about how you can challenge yourself, encouraging self-reflection and critical analysis when working in asset management. Once you have consumed it, you will want to dip in and out as an aide memoir to support your delivery plan.'
— **Daniella Barrow,** Senior Director of Norse Consulting

'Essential reading for the local government or public sector asset management professional, providing a wealth of practical advice and approaches. A really useful and logical guide. If only it had been published earlier!'
— **Paul Kettrick,** Head of Invest Falkirk, Falkirk Council

The Property Strategy Handbook

Building a
Local Authority
Property Strategy
in Six Easy Steps

CHRIS BRAIN

Re^think

First published in Great Britain in 2022
by Rethink Press (www.rethinkpress.com)

© Copyright Chris Brain

All rights reserved. No part of this publication may be reproduced, stored in or introduced into a retrieval system, or transmitted, in any form, or by any means (electronic, mechanical, photocopying, recording or otherwise) without the prior written permission of the publisher.

The right of Chris Brain to be identified as the author of this work has been asserted by him in accordance with the Copyright, Designs and Patents Act 1988.

This book is sold subject to the condition that it shall not, by way of trade or otherwise, be lent, resold, hired out, or otherwise circulated without the publisher's prior consent in any form of binding or cover other than that in which it is published and without a similar condition including this condition being imposed on the subsequent purchaser.

This book is dedicated to Sue.

Throughout a long part of my career, she has been the most supportive wife I could have wished for. In my pre-qualification days, she encouraged me to gain my professional qualification in order for me to secure career progression. When I moved to CIPFA, which involved lots of work, travel and nights away from home every week, she supported me. And when in 2019 I decided I would like to form my own business, she was again right by my side, and remains so to this day.

Contents

Introduction	1
PART ONE Preparing The Ground	**9**
1 The 6 Ps Method	**11**
Context	11
Asset management plan vs corporate property strategy	13
What is a corporate property strategy?	15
The origins of the 6 Ps	17
Summary	19
2 Mobilisation	**21**
6 Ps summary	22
The big prize	27
Project planning	28
Preparing others	30

Involving stakeholders	31
Information gathering	39
Summary	40

PART TWO The 6 Ps Method — 41

3 Portfolio — 43

Dimensions: Portfolio size and form	44
Detail: Portfolio segments	52
Dangers: Portfolio SWOT	57
Top tips	62
Summary	63

4 Purpose — 65

Desire: Bringing clarity	66
Direction: Organisational alignment	76
Deliverables: Expectation criteria	82
Top tips	85
Summary	85

5 Performance — 87

Destination: Setting performance areas	89
Discharge: Establishing current performance	96
Data: Performance and data gaps	100

	Top tips	107
	Summary	107
6	**Policies**	**109**
	Divergence: Missing policies	111
	Departure: Policy non-compliance	120
	Devise: Developing new policy	123
	Top tips	126
	Summary	127
7	**People**	**129**
	Dexterity: Designing around capabilities	130
	Design: Getting the structure right	135
	Development: Allow your people to grow	140
	Top tips	144
	Summary	144
8	**Process**	**145**
	Delivery: Strengthening operating procedures	147
	Decisions: Strengthening governance	151
	Databank: Tools of the trade	160
	Top tips	163
	Summary	164

PART THREE Getting It Done   **165**

  9 **Making A Start**   **167**

      First night nerves   167

      Action, not hope   170

      Priorities   171

      Check your bearings   173

      Corporate property strategy structure   174

      Summary   175

Conclusion   **177**

      The 6Ps in practice   179

References   **183**

Acknowledgements   **185**

The Author   **189**

Introduction

If the eyes are the window to the soul, a local authority's property portfolio and how it is managed is a window into the wider organisation. Where I see a good and well-maintained local authority property portfolio, I see a good, well-run, modern local authority.

The corporate property strategy is a key aspect of that window. A cohesive strategic approach to the management of these often disparate property portfolios says a lot about the organisation that created it. A strategy must be dynamic and flexible enough to support the delivery of a combination of corporate objectives, service objectives and cross-cutting strategies within a challenging financial environment.

Without a corporate property strategy, you are borrowing from the future to pay for today. Put another way, you are sacrificing what you most need for your immediate want.

The Property Strategy Handbook is a ground-breaking practical tool for anyone in local government struggling with the process of writing a corporate property strategy. Framed around my unique 6 Ps methodology, it is the first of its kind to offer this level of pragmatic information and will be an immense support as you create, develop and refresh your strategy. I wish it had been around for me when I was a new and struggling asset manager.

Many public sector organisations can easily find themselves in what I call the 'asset management wilderness'. They may not realise they are in a wilderness, but they are stagnant and not making progress. Sometimes, they may slip backwards into what I call the danger zone (see diagram below) where there is no strategic asset management happening at all.

INTRODUCTION

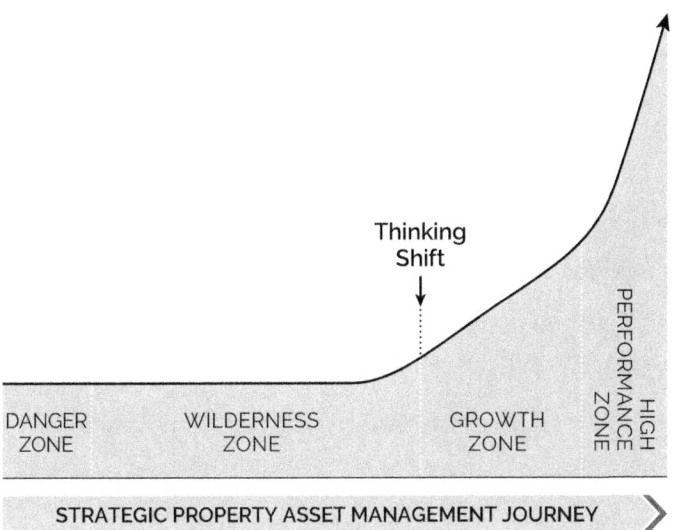

The asset management wilderness

Being in the wilderness zone is not a bad thing, it is part of the strategic property asset management journey, but being in that zone for too long is harmful as damaging practices, habits and behaviours become embedded.

You know you are in the wilderness zone when some of the following apply to your organisation:

- There are missing pieces to your strategic management of property
- There is an unfounded belief the organisation makes strategic property decisions

- The property portfolio is having little tangible positive impact
- The way property is managed is detached from organisational strategies
- Portfolio performance lacks structure and ambition
- There is no real grasp of the property portfolio and its purpose
- There is no clear property policy framework
- There is insufficient resource capacity to deliver your property priorities

To get out of the wilderness zone, one needs a trigger. Adopting the 6 Ps methodology when you create your corporate property strategy can be such a trigger, dragging you out of the wilderness zone and into the growth zone and eventually into the high-performance zone. If you find yourself in the growth zone, you will see that:

- There is clarity on the property portfolio, and its purpose
- The portfolio has defined segments and is managed accordingly
- There is clear strategic direction for the performance of the portfolio
- The property portfolio is performing well

- There is a robust asset policy framework
- There are strong links between property strategy and the organisational policy and strategy framework
- The leadership team is fully engaged in property strategy

If tackled the wrong way, writing a corporate property strategy can be a lonely and challenging process. While one of the core elements of the strategic landscape, there isn't always the necessary time devoted to it and there can be uncertainty about what the document should look like, or where to start.

Local government is a high-pressure environment where strategy often takes a backseat to operational issues. Without a pre-set structure, time can be wasted trying different approaches, layouts and options. There may be nobody providing guidance on what your strategy should look like. The job is often left to the last minute, with tight deadlines for completion. Worse, your strategy is hastily developed, but is not implemented because of lack of resources, complexity or local politics. Sometimes, the process becomes a tick-box exercise and the strategy is then left on a dusty shelf.

This gives rise to one of the most frequent questions I have been asked by asset managers over the past twenty years. What is a 'good' corporate property strategy? There is no template readily available. Trawling the internet looking for other examples is often seen as the first quick fix. Plagiarism is rife. The resulting strategy can be a rushed, bland, poorly-structured document lacking uniqueness. The strategy often sets out the wrong direction and requires huge reworking during later drafting stages. It may be ignored by colleagues and elected members and so it will likely not bring about the transformation so often needed.

The second quick fix is getting someone else to write it for you. An external consultant often comes with a pre-determined structure in their head, thinking they know what a 'good' strategy looks like. Unless you choose well, this isn't the answer either. You don't need a pre-determined strategy. You need a strategy reflecting the uniqueness of your organisation, your communities, your neighbourhoods and your specific challenges. You don't need a strategy delivered to you like a take-away meal. You need one developed and owned by everyone in the organisation.

The 6 Ps methodology I describe in *The Property Strategy Handbook* will take you through a clear, step-by-step process you will not find anywhere else. As you work your way through my unique methodology (Portfolio, Purpose, Performance, Policies, People and Process), you will find it will do a great deal of the heavy lifting for you in writing your strategy. Each one of the 6 Ps lets you complete another piece of the property strategy puzzle. Each step of *The Property Strategy Handbook* will help you build a corporate property strategy that will clearly describe your organisation's unique challenges and desires. Your strategy will set out what aspects of strategic asset management are already in place and identify the gaps for you to work on over the duration of your strategy.

Local authorities have a long-held reputation for doing things slowly, but it doesn't have to be that way. *The Property Strategy Handbook* is the guide that will see you getting this daunting task off your desk in far less time than you thought possible. It draws upon a wealth of experience, successes and failures I have accumulated during my career and is packed with case studies which enlighten and show you the path to your unique corporate property strategy. The sector has been crying out for a structured system like this for far too long. I hope you will be excited by *The Property Strategy Handbook* and find it valuable, not only for its core purpose of writing a corporate property strategy, but also as a learning and development tool for your team and others across your organisation.

How to read this book

The book is in three parts. Part One helps you to prepare the ground – both for yourself and others – before you start working through the 6 Ps methodology. Part Two takes you through the 6 Ps and is the 'meat' of the book. Part Three provides some advice on how to get the process implemented.

I encourage you to read the book slowly. Have something you can scribble notes in as you work your way through it and highlight passages which stand out for you. Ideally, pause a while between sections or chapters to make sure you understand the concepts and any practical challenges they may pose.

When you finally implement the 6 Ps process in your organisation, if the methodology is ingrained, implementation will be faster and more effective. Slow down to speed up.

It is important to note that there is a deliberate sequence to the six key steps in methodology so don't be tempted to simply turn to the section that covers your particular organisational weakness. It may be helpful to dip into certain areas at a later stage, but it is important that you first read the handbook from beginning to end.

PART ONE
PREPARING THE GROUND

There is much to prepare before you start writing a corporate property strategy. Like any journey, if you set off just a few degrees out from where you should, your eventual destination will not be the place you intended. Don't be tempted to skip the next two chapters in your impatience to get to the 6 Ps methodology.

ONE
The 6 Ps Method

Before I expose you to the detail of the methodology (Chapters 3 to 8), I need to clear up any confusion about what a corporate property strategy is, and what it is not. It might also help for you to know how the 6 Ps methodology came about, and how important it is you approach it in the right way.

Context

Local authorities are an essential part of the fabric of UK society. They provide a wide range of statutory and discretionary services from teaching our children and looking after the vulnerable through to supporting the health and wellbeing of all our communities and providing emergency services such as police and fire.

Funding available to local authorities has reduced in real terms over a long period of time. In England, for example, government-funded spending power to local authorities reduced by 52.3% between 2010–2011 and 2020–2021.[1] They are regularly expected to do more with less, and they are not the masters of their funding fate.

Many of the services that local authorities provide rely on the use or ownership of physical property assets. A great deal of public money is tied up in, consumed by, and can be generated through, the ownership and control of those assets. The balance sheet value of local authority land and buildings exceeds £382 billion.[2] These assets represent more than money; they are at the heart of local government. Now, more than ever before, it is essential the public has reliable assurance about how local government bodies use, and account for, their resources.

Local government is special because its roots are in places, and places really matter to people and communities. Places offer a sense of identity and attachment.

Property resources touch all service delivery in varying degrees, and services should be actively engaged to ensure alignment between the views of the property team and your service delivery teams. If property savings and modernisation can take pressure off wider cuts, or deliver better fit-for-purpose assets, then there is the opportunity for a win/win situation.

Local authority property portfolios are often extensive, comprising a mix of operational facilities, community facilities and commercial holdings. Throw into that mix a sprinkling of heritage assets, farms and assets used by traded services (such as ports, airports and housing companies), and the local authority land holding can be complex.

How local authorities use, manage and maintain their land and buildings has a direct impact on people and business in the community. They need a clear property strategy which recognises the financial envelope, acknowledges the increased demand for services and helps the organisation meet stringent net zero carbon targets. Local authority property portfolios have often expanded over generations, with some properties being no longer relevant and others repurposed so many times that they cease to be fit for purpose.

Asset management plan vs corporate property strategy

A 'corporate property strategy' is different to an 'asset management plan'. In the evolutionary cycle of strategic property asset management, nobody should put pen to paper on the asset management plan until they have a corporate property strategy in place.

An asset management plan can be an important document, but far too much time over the past decades has been focused on it as a corporate document. What matters is not the plan, but the planning. Too many asset plans are, in truth, a mixture of strategy and delivery. The Royal Institution of Chartered Surveyors (RICS) guidance[3] defines an asset management plan as, 'The delivery plan for property assets giving details such as timescales for action, costs (and revenues), outcomes to be achieved and responsibilities for action.' The RICS suggest this should be refreshed annually.

All too often, asset management plans are created without adequate strategy development. If asset management plans are created without adequate planning, they are next to useless. They will contain a series of unfunded and under-resourced ambitions (or sometimes no ambitions at all). There will be no proper structure or pathway setting out how things will be achieved. There will be no strategic direction aligned to corporate goals. Worst of all, there will be no appreciation of challenges or ownership of solutions. In short, it will be an aspirational document lacking substance and will not be implemented.

An asset management plan cannot exist in isolation. It cannot exist in a vacuum. Something must come before it, and that is the 'corporate property strategy'. The RICS asset management guidance from 2021[4] acknowledges this. It describes what it calls the asset management strategy as a 'strategic business planning document that indicates the direction of travel for asset management'. It is the step before thinking about the delivery plan. Despite this, it is a step often overlooked in the process. When that happens, the asset management plan is not built on strong foundations. It can later be undermined and will most likely underperform.

Many ask too much of the humble asset management plan. They expect it to be both the delivery plan and the strategy document rolled into one. That rarely works, and is one of the reasons asset management often has little traction in local authorities.

What is a corporate property strategy?

A corporate property strategy provides strategic direction. It orientates the organisation into how it wants its property assets to be managed, how it expects them to perform, and puts in place the governance structure within which property asset management can flourish. It is a framework for aligning corporate strategy and assets with performance and decision-making.

The corporate property strategy is not about the property assets, per se. It is not a document telling the reader which assets are performing well, or not so well. It will not tell you which properties should be retained, refurbished or sold. It will not tell you which buildings people should be sat in, or which buildings are now surplus. It will not identify property assets to be acquired. As important as all those issues are, they are not strategic issues. They have no place in a corporate property strategy. They do have their place in the asset management plan. The problem is that many jump straight to the asset management plan, setting out how the organisation is going to face all those challenges, without first establishing their strategic direction or orientation. That is what the corporate property strategy does.

The more that people can be convinced of the need to have a corporate property strategy, the better the resulting quality of asset management plans. Better asset management plans bring better assets, in the right locations. In turn, this provides the best possible support to local communities, improves the way public services are delivered, and makes those services more accessible. It also makes people happier in the workplace and supports them in it rather than holding them back. The corporate property strategy provides a high-level, long-term framework for the management and decision-making on property assets.

The strategy will be informed by:

- Considerations around the authority's involvement in, and support for, the local economy
- The implications of national or regional government policy decisions
- Commercial considerations
- Environmental aims
- Outsourcing policy and workforce strategy
- Service department aims

The corporate property strategy should lift eyes above and beyond what properties you currently own or occupy. It should focus on what the organisational aspirations are and how the property portfolio can, and will, support those initiatives and outcomes.

The origins of the 6 Ps

I created this six-step methodology in direct response to the failure by many to appreciate the role and importance of a good property strategy. I have drawn from personal experience in developing property strategies and asset management approaches for local authorities.

The roots of the methodology probably go back over twenty years, influenced by successes and failures along the way. Only recently did I stand back from those experiences and begin to analyse more deeply and seek to find a pattern in them.

Through that process I identified six vital ingredients for every corporate property strategy. Not only did I identify the ingredients, but I also unlocked the equally important sequence and interdependence of those elements. That lightbulb moment drove me to write this book, and share it with you.

By following each of the steps in the 6 Ps sequence, you can identify where you are doing well and where you can improve. As well as being sequential, the 6 Ps are also self-supporting. Imagine a tall ship with huge sails. Those sails have an immense weight and it is normally impossible for the ship's crew to lift any one of them. The answer is a block and tackle system. By running the ropes through a series of pulleys, the weight of the sail needs less force to lift it into position. The heavier the sail, the more pulleys needed for the crew to lift it. Now imagine the 6 Ps methodology as a series of six pulleys (see diagram below). If you skip one or more of the Ps, the weight in creating your corporate property strategy will become heavier and you will find it harder to exit the asset management wilderness zone.

THE 6 PS METHOD

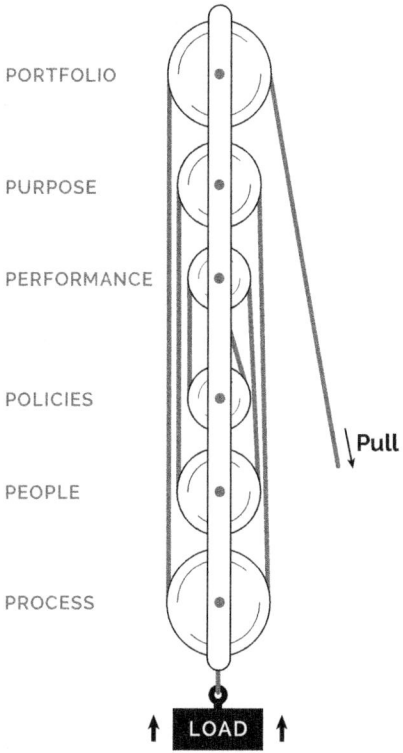

The 6 Ps as a series of pulleys

Summary

In this chapter, I have explained the difference between a corporate property strategy and an asset management plan. I have also explained the importance of having a corporate property strategy in place before attempting to write your asset management plan.

By following my recommended approach, you will have your best chance yet of writing a solid corporate property strategy and creating an environment where your organisation can be great at strategic property asset management.

TWO
Mobilisation

You are now clear on what a corporate property strategy is, and the important role it plays in embedding a strategic approach to property asset management in your organisation. In Chapter 3, you will start to work through my 6 Ps methodology to build your corporate property strategy, but first some preparation is needed. You need to prepare your mindset for the task. You also need to prepare others for their role in the process, because developing a corporate property strategy needs collaborative effort.

Creating a great corporate property strategy requires a methodical approach. Your corporate property strategy needs to have structure and follow a particular sequence. The sequence of the 6 Ps is important because they fall into two distinct categories. The first three are the 'push' Ps: they push you and the organisation to think differently about your property portfolio. The second set of three Ps are 'pull' Ps: they pull you towards your ambition for your property portfolio.

Pushing you and the organisation to change how you think about the property portfolio.

Pulling the organisation to deliver the change needed to meet your portfolio ambitions.

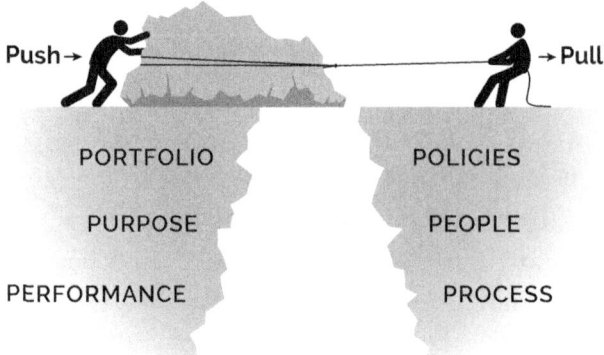

The push and pull of the 6 Ps

6 Ps summary

Below is a brief summary of each of the 6 Ps and an explanation as to why they are in this particular sequence.

Portfolio

Before you even begin to draft a corporate property strategy, you have to understand the property portfolio and its various property types or segments. A segment is a group of property assets with characteristics in common (such as core frontline service delivery assets). This is an absolute necessity, and yet it is a step often skipped over. After all, the property portfolio owned and operated by your organisation is what the strategy is to focus on. You cannot possibly develop a strategy for something you do not understand, and too few local authorities truly understand their property portfolio.

Often, local authority property portfolios have been inherited from predecessor authorities, rather than having been deliberately acquired. Sometimes an authority may have little clue how some properties came to be in the portfolio at all. Rarely has a property portfolio gone through a detailed review to establish what's in it, what it's for and how suitable it is for the delivery of modern services, now or in the future.

Purpose

Once you are clear on what your particular property portfolio comprises, you can begin to sketch out the purpose of each asset type, part or segment. If you have not taken the time to fully understand the portfolio, then defining purpose will be more difficult.

If you cannot define the purpose of each part of your portfolio, then it will be challenging to establish a performance management framework for the portfolio. It is performance measurement that tells you how you are doing. Establishing a clear purpose for each asset segment and individual asset will tell you quite a bit about how close you are to having the right property portfolio.

Performance

Many asset managers develop KPIs and other performance systems without first establishing the purpose of each asset, part or portfolio segment of the property portfolio. This is a big mistake.

You cannot decide what to measure if you don't know why you are measuring it, and how measuring it delivers great performance. Many people waste a lot of time measuring and reporting against the wrong matrices or with the wrong performance dashboard (or 'balanced scorecard') because they have not linked it to their portfolio purpose. When you know what you are measuring, and for what purpose, you can then establish a clear set of property policies that will help you deliver that performance and purpose.

Policies

Developing a robust performance management framework allows you to achieve your ambitions for your property portfolio, but you need further help. You need all those interacting with the property portfolio to play by the same rules in meeting performance aspirations. A framework of property-related policies will provide structure to your purpose and performance by providing the support system to both day-to-day and strategic decisions made on the property portfolio.

People

With a clear portfolio performance, backed by a robust performance management framework and property policy framework, you will be in a position to organise your people in a way that will deliver your strategic property goals.

No organisational structure sits in a vacuum. Your people resources are key to you achieving your ambitions for your property portfolio. If the staff resource is not well aligned to your priorities, you will fall short. This is not just about the property team. The organisational structure in these terms includes everyone involved in management and decisions around the property portfolio – your property board, service managers, directors, management team and elected members.

Property is an organisational resource: while property professionals know more about technical aspects, services know more about how the accommodation works for their service delivery.

Process

To have your people resources operating as an effective, well-oiled machine, you need clear processes. Even the best group of people will flounder if the processes by which strategic or operational decisions are made are not robust.

Decisions are being made on your property portfolio every working minute. The people making those decisions need a clear 'route map' to follow. It can help if your organisation has adopted quality management standards, but even then, these won't save you from bad decisions if there is poor or absent strategy or people are not 'living' the strategy.

Operational decisions, for example, a building surveyor deciding which boiler to install or a valuer deciding whether to offer a new tenant a rent-free period, are routinely made. If there is no clear process to align with purpose, performance and policies, then wrong decisions will be made. It is not just operational decisions, though. The same goes for bigger, strategic decisions, for example, your property board having to choose whether a particular site should be used to erect starter business units, develop affordable housing, build an energy farm or create a mixed-use commercial scheme.

The big prize

Perhaps you've never thought about property strategy in these 6 Ps terms before and my lightbulb moment is now creating a similar lightbulb moment for you. Maybe it was something you were also instinctively aware of, but also never formalised. You may now be appreciating why your organisation remains in the asset management wilderness zone. Perhaps you have paid attention to some of the Ps, but not all of them. Hopefully you are already starting to see where things may have gone wrong for you in the past. While this is progress, you need to keep your eye on the prize.

The prize is not the corporate property strategy itself. The prize could be any number of things which improve your property portfolio, and will vary from organisation to organisation. Examples may be:

- Better-managed property assets
- Clearer strategic direction for property assets
- Clearer operational property management parameters
- A clearer property policy framework
- Better governance and decision-making processes
- Clear performance ambitions
- Improved property data intelligence

- Skilled, capable staff resources that deliver efficient, effective processes

Even these are not the ultimate prize. The ultimate prize is more effective and efficient public services that support your local communities well and make customers happy. That is the prime role of any public body like yours. Your organisation's property portfolio can make a huge impact on that. Good property assets support service delivery. It may not make it better, but poor property assets will most certainly negatively impact service delivery.

You must resist distractions during the process of preparing and developing your corporate property strategy, or you will never get it written. You need to move at pace during this process. Identify where there are gaps in information or knowledge and the other areas I share with you, make a note of them, and come back to them during the strategy implementation, *not* during the strategy development.

Project planning

Writing a corporate property strategy is a project. Like any other project, it takes good preparation to pull it off. As the saying goes, 'Failure to plan means planning to fail.' The tasks throughout the remainder of this book will help you to keep a structured approach to this project. The sequence to those tasks provides a framework for a programme of actions and activities. What the framework does not do is provide life's most precious resource: time.

Creating your corporate property strategy will take time. A lot of it. You need time to think, time to plan, time to reflect, time to facilitate and time to implement and write. It is not just your time. You also need the precious time of others. (Later in this chapter I will suggest a process to help you to maximise the motivation of others to get involved in this project and establish a coalition of the willing.)

Those who are going to support you through this project will also need to maintain motivation for the entire journey. You do not want to surprise them along the way with new tasks. You need to plan out the project so everyone involved (you included) knows what this project is going to take, what the key stages of the project are, how much time they are having to give you, what thinking they will need to do and how it all fits together. You need to set out who is going to be doing what, and when. You need to get dates in diaries for interviews, meetings, board meetings, group discussions and facilitated workshops. This project is going to involve all of these.

Like all projects, it will need project management. You have a few choices here. If your organisation has a programme management team, they may be able to provide resources, skills or support. You could also consider appointing a project manager (some organisations have in-house ones). Project management is a specialist skill in its own right, and affords some independence to facilitate the involvement of other disciplines outside of the property function. I am not going to suggest any specific project planning tool. There are a number of proprietary ones on the market and everyone will have their favourite.

Preparing others

As well as preparing yourself and the project, you need to prepare others. Writing a corporate property strategy is not a task to be tackled alone. Sure, one person has to carry the weight of the drafting and has to be the driving force throughout the process by leading the project, but if you believe this project will be like ploughing a lonely furrow, think again.

The corporate property strategy should be a collaborative effort, ideally reporting to a project sponsor. It is essential that the strategy is owned by everyone and all stakeholders have a part in shaping it. If not, then it will simply be regarded as a strategy that 'property' has created. In a phenomenon dubbed 'the IKEA effect',[5] researchers have found that people prefer things they help make to things that are pre-assembled, even if their creations are of lower quality. With ownership comes buy-in to the principles and the direction for the property portfolio. With ownership comes effectiveness. Some people may be content to see a strategy that has been written by someone else fail (and perhaps even take great pleasure from it). It is human nature. Such people are less likely to stand by and let a strategy struggle that they helped create.

When everyone involved in strategy development feels empowered, it creates a momentum. People work harder, innovate and become far more invested in the process. They bring agility of thought. They focus on solutions, not problems. Strategy objectives work against strategy execution because they're developed at an organisational level, but implementing them involves individuals across a number of service departments. If you share the development of the corporate property strategy, you will share the burden of implementation too. What applies to Swedish furniture also applies to corporate property strategy.

Involving stakeholders

Often, stakeholders are kept out of a property strategy process out of concern they will slow things down, that they know nothing about property strategy, but this is a short-sighted view. Your corporate property strategy is more likely to stick to its flight plan when those responsible for its ultimate delivery have a stake in defending it. Stakeholders can also bring insights into political motivations and values, into challenges different services are experiencing, challenges services face in meeting customer demands and numerous other aspects those within the property service may be blind to.

The questions you should be asking are: Who should I involve in the process, and how? (We will answer this as you work through Chapters 3 to 8.) You need to alert your stakeholders that you are writing a corporate property strategy so they are ready to provide the important feedback and active contributions you will be asking them for. Everyone needs to be clear that this strategy is going to happen and that it's better to be on the team and help prioritise identification and direction than to be sitting outside the process.

Every organisation has its own unique people structures, governance processes, dynamics, culture and way of doing things, so giving you a definitive list of your stakeholders is difficult. As a minimum, you should include board members, senior elected politicians, directors, service managers, senior property managers and operational property teams. You will need different people at different stages of following the 6 Ps methodology.

Some stakeholders might be involved in the project team (if you have one). Others will be involved less directly in the oversight of strategy development, but their contribution is equally valuable and will be key to creating a robust strategy. One thing to make clear to the stakeholders you will be engaging in this strategy process is that you do not want them to be bystanders. That is a mistaken belief too many have. Your stakeholders are part of the team, they are key players, and the strategy is as much theirs as yours. Everyone must bring themselves fully to the table. At times you might be asking them to lead on areas of strategy activities for you. Whatever you do, stress that they need to make time for this task ahead. This may be challenging, but even more so if they believe the corporate property strategy is nothing to do with them. It is your task to convince them otherwise.

If you have no previous experience of stakeholder engagement, there may be merit in using stakeholder mapping as a practical tool. This is a visual process of laying out all the stakeholders on a single map. The benefit of this approach is to produce a visual representation of all the people who can influence your project, and how they are connected.

Motivating stakeholders

Newton's First Law of Motion says an object at rest stays at rest, and an object in motion stays in motion, with the same speed, and in the same direction, unless acted upon by an unbalanced force.[6] In other words, if things are stagnant, they will stay stagnant until something happens to change it. If things are deteriorating or improving, they will carry on that way, unless an opposite force comes along to change it. If we want our corporate property strategy to bring about change, we would do well to heed Newton's Law and think about how we bring that change about.

CASE STUDY: STAKEHOLDER ENGAGEMENT

I was working with a client a few years ago to produce a new asset management plan for them. We were keen to get broad engagement with as many stakeholders as possible, so we decided to run a series of facilitated discussion sessions with elected members. We put a couple of dates in the diary and invitations were sent out to every member. They were free to attend the date that suited them best.

Out of the fifty-five elected councillors, only two attended the first date. On the second date, the number was slightly higher due to some poking and prodding by council officers, but still appalling.

The lesson out of that experience is that it takes two to engage. Asset management planning is not the most exciting topic to most people. Councillors are busy people, working hard to support and represent their communities. They need to prioritise their time. They cannot get involved with everything they are asked to, so you need to provide them with the motivation to engage.

Each stakeholder is a potential change agent. They are also an individual with their own personal objectives or motivations. You must identify these and then encourage each of them to identify the achievement of those objectives with a great corporate property strategy. Find a way for them to recognise the corporate property strategy as a solution to some of their problems, pain points or irritations.

Before you approach anyone to be part of this journey, I recommend creating a simple table on a blank sheet of paper or on a Word document. In the first column, list the names of your stakeholders. Think about each person in turn. What do you know of them and their main motivations? Have their interactions with you revealed anything about them as an individual and what drives them? Some people are motivated by work outcomes or personal achievements and some by other, much wider global principles. Try to identify at least three of these motivations or objectives for each of your stakeholders and list these in a second column next to each of their names.

Next, apply your mind to what pain you believe they are suffering in terms of that motivation, as regards either the nature, characteristics or performance of the organisation's property portfolio, or the way that portfolio is managed. This needs to be sharp pain, like a papercut or a splinter that constantly niggles or frustrates them. It will be those things they might have mentioned to you in the past, or you have heard them talk about with others. It may be something they keep returning to time and time again and about which nothing ever really changes. Ideally, you need to find three pain points, at least one for each of the three motivations or objectives you previously identified. Write these pain points on your sheet in a third column.

At this stage, you will ideally have identified nine pain points for each stakeholder, as shown in the example below. You should not infer from this table that the equivalent person in your organisation would have the same motivations and pain points, as these will vary from person to person and organisation to organisation. It is simply here to demonstrate the suggested approach.

STAKEHOLDER	MOTIVATIONS	PAIN POINTS
Stakeholder 1 (Finance Director)	1. Balanced budget	a. Reductions in external financial support
		b. Rising service operating costs
		c. Rising energy costs
	2. Well-funded and efficient capital programme	a. Capital wasted on the wrong projects
		b. Delayed receipts from property disposals
		c. Capital project over-runs
	3. Recognition for prudent financial management	a. Rental income 'lost' through discounted third sector rents
		b. High commercial rent arrears
		c. Short-term political focus

Now the exciting part. In a final column alongside each of the pain points, identify the thing the corporate property strategy will do for them and their pain point. Think in terms of how the drafting process or the corporate property strategy will deliver or create to either ease or remove that pain point for that person. Some people's pain will be the overall organisational structure or culture. You may feel the corporate property strategy can do little to bring about change in those areas, but a corporate property strategy can be a domino that tips other dominoes. Don't underestimate the power of starting a journey of strategic planning and thinking.

This might result in a table that looks a bit like the one below.

You might need to be creative, but please do work carefully through this process. Think deep and hard about each person, what drives them and what solutions they will see from the eventual property strategy. That time spent will pay dividends.

You will use what you generate when you reach out to your stakeholders to seek their engagement in the creation of the corporate property strategy. The more they believe the new strategy will solve their problems and pain points and meet their motivations and objectives, the more they will engage. The more they engage, the better the strategy will be. The better the strategy is, the more chance there is it will be delivered.

STAKEHOLDER	MOTIVATIONS	PAIN POINTS	PROPERTY STRATEGY SOLUTION
Stakeholder 1 (Finance Director)	1. Balanced budget	a. Reductions in external financial support b. Rising service operating costs c. Rising energy costs	a. Increase commercial property income b. Clear asset retention rationale c. Improve energy efficiency
	2. Well-funded and efficient capital programme	a. Capital wasted on the wrong projects b. Delayed receipts from property disposals c. Capital project over-runs	a. Business cases linked to property vision b. Disposal programme which is deliverable c. Prioritisation of resources
	3. Recognition for prudent financial management	a. Rental income 'lost' through discounted third sector rents b. High commercial rent arrears c. Short-term political focus	a. Policy on property disposal at less than best consideration b. Rent collection and enforcement procedures c. Strategic property objectives

Information gathering

You are close to starting the process of building your corporate property strategy, but before you can begin the task, you need to spend some time mobilising and gathering information. Some of this information will be close at hand; some will be further from your reach.

You may well delegate the gathering task to others, but you need to decide what information needs to be gathered. The information needed will vary in detail from organisation to organisation. There is, however, a broad pattern to what you will need and this gathering process needs to start early to give you time to refine your information requirements. That way, when you come to use the information, it is in the shape and form to make strategy building efficient and effective.

This should include gathering together all relevant organisational plans, policies and strategies, whether in draft or adopted. This might include organisational plans, operational delivery plans, service plans and service strategies. It should also include the current property policies in place, core property data, property performance data, service reviews underway, proposed changes to service delivery or operating models, forthcoming changes to outsourcing/insourcing, etc; in short, anything that could impact on your corporate property strategy.

In particular, you should distil from all these service and organisation strategies and plans any areas where your corporate property strategy can support the ambitions and priorities contained in them. Alongside this you should seek to identify issues impacting the property portfolio from these strategies and plans. Ideally, schedule these out as you will find that valuable when you get to Chapter 4.

Summary

The process of creating a corporate property strategy should be approached as a project. It is not something written in a dark room by someone from the property team, but a collaborative task involving multiple players. You are now ready to begin working through the core of the book: my 6 Ps methodology. I hope that you are as excited by the prospect as I am for you. By following this methodology, you can create a truly great corporate property strategy.

PART TWO
THE 6 PS METHOD

In Part Two, we get into the meat of the 6 Ps methodology. You already know what each of the 6 Ps are. As I detail them in turn, you will appreciate why they are each as important as one another and how they relate to one another.

THREE
Portfolio

Before you tackle a corporate property strategy, the vital first step is to fully understand the property portfolio – your land holdings and your buildings. It is a step many miss out, which is why so many corporate property strategies go awry.

The first two parts of this chapter will take you through a process to cleanse your property database and make it fit for asset strategy. The final part will help you to identify the key risks and opportunities your property portfolio presents early on in the strategy development process.

There are three elements to the Portfolio step:

1. Dimensions: Portfolio size and form

2. Detail: Portfolio segments
3. Dangers: Portfolio SWOT

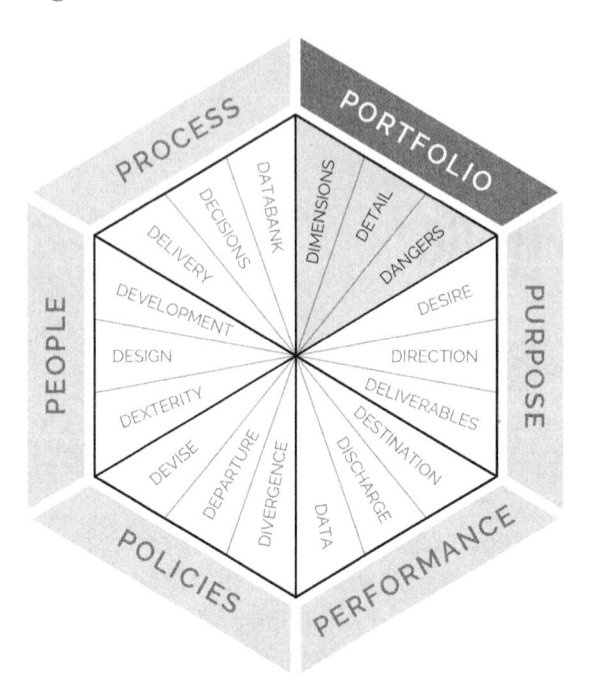

Dimensions: Portfolio size and form

Most local authorities do not truly understand their property portfolio. Property databases and GIS systems have been around long enough to be complete, especially if you have been through a voluntary Land Registration process, but it is still possible to discover assets you own have been left off the records. Because asset databases and records are so cluttered, it can be difficult to get a feel for the portfolio as a whole.

A few years ago, I was undertaking an asset valuation data audit for a council client and during the project I discovered their most valuable asset had been missed off their balance sheet. It is a landmark asset that most people in the UK would recognise instantly from a photograph, and yet it was missing from the database and had been for a number of years. I know of countless other similar examples. It shouldn't happen, but it does.

The importance of understanding your property portfolio

To create an effective corporate property strategy, you simply must know what property assets the organisation owns or occupies, their size and their form. Some might say you could begin developing a strategy without understanding your portfolio, as the important thing is the portfolio you are aiming for. While I appreciate this view, it is not a course I recommend. While the corporate property strategy is a forward-looking document, it must recognise where you are now. Often, this can be more important because for many local authorities the finances and other resources necessary to make wholesale changes to the property portfolio will be limited.

Local authority property portfolios have often grown organically over many decades – some of it acquired (not always out of choice), some of it donated, and some of it inherited. Your property teams may believe they know the portfolio, and they probably have the best chance of doing so, but even then, different parts of the property teams will have visibility on different parts of the portfolio. Others around the authority will have far less knowledge of the whole portfolio, and your corporate property strategy is an organisational document that will demand collaboration. There has to be a levelling up of portfolio knowledge at the start of the project.

Streamlining property asset categorisation

Over the past three decades, local authority property records have come a long way. Local authorities have moved from physical card-and-paper mapping systems to digitised mapping layers linked to asset management databases. Property assets have been categorised to be able to be captured by these digital systems, but digital systems are built by digital people. Those people are IT experts, not property experts. Databases are structured to allow as many property categories as organisations need. That all sounds helpful, but it isn't. Databases rarely have an eye for property strategy and the need for meaningful asset categories.

These databases are then put in the hands of property professionals. Property professionals can be sticklers for detail. Any good general practice surveyor could bore you for hours on the difference between a licence, a tenancy and a lease or the difference between a licence, an easement and a wayleave.

This 'perfect storm' combination of IT and property professionals devising and populating asset databases has resulted in most databases having a multitude of property asset categories. This huge number of categories might be legally accurate, but it does not serve property strategy well.

One of the first tasks I generally set a new consultancy client is to provide me with a list of their property assets. It is rare for my heart not to sink when I receive such a list. It is not the length of the list or the number of 'assets' that causes me pain, but the number of asset categories. There are always far too many.

CASE STUDY: DATA DISCIPLINE

At the early stage of supporting one local authority client to write a new asset management plan, I was sent a spreadsheet of all the property assets they owned or operated from. This was a unitary authority, with around 1,100 lines taken from the managed records section of their asset database.

Of those 1,100 or so records, there were 435 where the cell was blank under the 'usage description' heading. In other words, in nearly 40% of the data lines, there was no information in the database as to how this asset was being used.

> Interestingly, there were around thirty assets with a description of a garage. Of those, only seven had a usage description of garage. The others were blank, showing a likelihood of incomplete data. In other examples, what were clearly industrial business units carried asset use descriptions of either 'industrial unit' or 'commercial', or were left blank. Some sub-stations were described as 'sub-stations', others as 'commercial'.
>
> In short, there was a complete lack of discipline of the allocation of asset usage descriptions.

The length of time it takes to get a true picture of the property portfolio has nothing to do with the quality of the database, and everything to do with how people have classified and described property assets. When given the freedom to do so, property teams will bring a precision to property categorisation that is unnecessary.

Miscellaneous is good

Over the years I have seen organisations seek to bring clarity to the dimensions of the property portfolio by ditching the 'miscellaneous' asset category. By doing so, IT people and property managers alike believe they are doing the right thing, but they are not. These miscellaneous assets might include sub-stations, easements, wayleaves, fuel storage, meter boxes – all manner of stuff that is too long a list to include here.

They have never been important to me when I have written a corporate property strategy. I have never heard anyone else say they are important, either. I am not advocating removing these assets from the database. All I am talking about is thinking about the way you classify them, to bring strategic clarity which will benefit not only the property strategy, but also the capital strategy.

That clarity will be of similar benefit in operational management too, especially when it comes to understanding the demands of the portfolio and dealing with things like prioritised maintenance and premises compliance. A cluttered property database creates lack of clarity and impedes decision-making. The property database is a hugely important tool, but people often forget it is a tool for strategic management as well as day-to-day operational management. The right balance needs to be struck so information is structured to serve both purposes, not just the latter.

You simply must understand the dimensions and nature of the portfolio. What is in it, how many of each type of asset you have, and reducing the number of asset categories. You will feel much better about yourself if you do this. It will be a bit like how you feel when you tidy your desk or sort out your sock drawer – except sorting out your portfolio has a much bigger payoff. If you felt you didn't understand the portfolio before, this will bring you real clarity.

Property category descriptions

In one asset list I received recently from a client, play areas carried a property type description of 'land'. This same property type description of 'land' was also used for a whole range of completely different assets. This included a former public convenience, development sites, a recycling point, a mine shaft, a maintenance depot, allotments, grazing land, a former caravan park, a quarry, common land, a community learning centre, a beach and a surgery under construction.

Given that wide range of assets with the same property type category, what is it they have in common? Yes, they all are (or appear to be) land assets, but in terms of developing a property strategy, that isn't necessarily helpful. That's what I mean by structuring your property data to support your strategy. I would suggest in this particular case, what separated these assets was more important than what they had in common, and the application of property type category of 'land' needs reviewing.

In that same asset list, there was a nursery described as 'retail', a radio mast described as 'industrial' and a bus station described as 'infrastructure'. This particular database is crying out for some renewed discipline, but it will not be alone. If you review your database, I am confident you will find similar examples.

CASE STUDY: DATA DESCRIPTIONS

One police authority I once worked with didn't have the issue of large numbers of assets. I was provided with an asset list at the start of the project to write a new estates strategy. There were only 140 or so lines in the spreadsheet.

One might have thought with such an understandably small portfolio, the scope for lack of clarity was much reduced. Well, so it was. But there did remain some lack of clarity.

In developing the strategy, what we needed to know was not whether any particular asset was a police station, but what sort of station it was. There are a number of different types of police station, and this was important in first reporting the different numbers of types of assets in the strategy.

Police stations were described as either 'offices', 'station', 'NHP station', 'NHP office' or 'station with custody'. That is five different descriptions for a police station. What was actually important in building the estates strategy was which of these were actually stations. It turns out that one was not even a station anymore. Of the remainder, we needed to simply know which of the stations were open to the public. This was the important information for the strategy to have, but we didn't have it. Being such a small property portfolio, it didn't take much effort to create an extra column in the spreadsheet to record it. The client now has this information at its fingertips, where beforehand the information was in people's heads.

The case study above is far from unique. I have seen countless examples of property data that muddle asset type with asset use or service department titles. Many property databases will have data fields such as property name, property type, directorate, directorate division, asset category, category division and sub-category division or something similar. How you populate those fields is critical to developing a strategic knowledge of the portfolio. In many situations, these fields are not used well and there is often a lack of discipline to property descriptors used within each field.

Detail: Portfolio segments

With the clarity that database cleansing brings, the next step is to segment the portfolio so you can understand its strategic parts. After all, if you don't know what you own, there can be no truly effective strategy for managing it.

Creating your segments

Say, for example, after the first step you had a property type descriptor of 'Offices'. You will likely have a number of different types of offices held and used for different purposes and outcomes. While it is possible you might at some point want to know what the total number of offices are in your portfolio; you are more likely to want to know what different types of office you have. That is of more strategic value.

What you need is a data category hierarchy structure that allows you to group together all buildings held for the same purpose, or which have strategic characteristics in common. Flexibility and having a data structure that allows you to draw valuable strategic data that will serve strategic reviews and management is key. If you are undertaking a strategic review of your administrative offices, you may or may not want to include offices leased to others, where these are held for commercial or investment purposes. You need the flexibility to do both.

In the table below, I have recreated a typical database structure. It may not be identical to your database, but should be similar. There are five assets in the table. Each one is an office, but not all offices are the same. The database needs to recognise their differences. The portfolio segments need to be structured to allow you to manage the portfolio and the segments strategically. Here are descriptions to explain what each of the assets is, and how the nature of that asset should affect how it is described in the database:

- Property A: Main civic centre HQ
- Property B: An operational housing area office
- Property C: Let to a third party purely for the rate of return
- Property D: Let to a local small business on flexible terms
- Property E: Vacant former operational office

Property Name	Property Type	Directorate	Directorate Division	Accounting Category	Accounting Division	Sub-category
Property A	Office	Corporate services	Property	Other land and buildings	Operational	
Property B	Office	Neighbourhoods	Housing	Other land and buildings	Operational	
Property C	Office	Corporate services	Property	Investment property	Non-operational	
Property D	Office	Community services	Regeneration	Other land and buildings	Operational	
Property E	Office	Corporate services	Property	Surplus	Non-operational	

Hopefully this simple example shows how database categorisation should work. Don't get hung up on the terminology I have chosen to use, yours may be different. The point of the example is to show what good differentiation and consistency looks like.

Similarly, if you had an asset category for leisure centres, you may not want to include leisure facilities that are not municipal (for example, leases to leisure businesses such as private gyms) in the same segment as municipal leisure facilities. At a broader level though, you might want libraries, leisure centres, shared service buildings and area housing offices within the same segment. These are distinct asset types. The buildings may be nothing alike. They may each perform a completely different purpose and are obviously distinct from one another. But what they do have in common is they may be regarded as core assets for delivering frontline services. In terms of property strategy, this means they have more in common than it might first seem. In developing a corporate property strategy, what these different assets have in common is more important than what they don't.

The purpose of this process is to arrive at a set of broad asset groupings distinct from one another. With these strategic segments identified, you can begin to see the wood for the trees. Suddenly, the true nature of the portfolio is clear, which makes strategy development so much easier.

Take another look at the 'Sub-category' column in the table above. I often see organisations not sure how to use this column. They hate to leave it empty, so they put something in it. The worst thing you can do (and which many do) is to simply repeat the descriptor from the 'Property Type' column. This is pointless and a waste of your database functionality. This column can be used to provide a strategic tag for each asset. The question to ask yourself is, 'What are my strategic segments, and how will I use this database functionality?' There are a number of ways to approach this. The right way is the way that works for you. Approach this task with careful thought and don't follow a structure just because someone else does so. You need to think about how you might want to report on your property portfolio in the future. It is an iterative process, and you may well revisit this process as you work through the Purpose and Performance steps.

Areas for you to consider might include whether the service operating from the asset is statutory or non-statutory (discretionary) or perhaps whether the service is client-facing or a back-office facility. It might be important to you to differentiate between residential facilities (such as care homes, staff accommodation or service tenancies) and non-residential facilities. For you, it might simply be about identifying core services from non-core services, however you define that. Your options are countless. As part of the process, you may start to stray into the second P (Purpose). This is quite normal, but just don't go too far into it. As mentioned earlier, if you have muddled asset categories, this will muddle your thinking on why you have the assets. If you are muddled on why you have the assets, you will be muddled on how you expect them to perform.

Dangers: Portfolio SWOT

Risk is not just about avoiding bad things. The third element to the Portfolio step is to map out some of the main challenges and opportunities associated with the portfolio. I am not suggesting detailed reports on individual property assets and their performance. This needs to be at a high level. It can be undertaken across the portfolio as a whole, or within each segment. For me, there is power in doing both. This will pull out the key issues that need to be highlighted in your corporate property strategy, both positive and negative.

One way to do this, which may be familiar to you, is using a SWOT analysis. A SWOT analysis generally involves consideration of both internal and external factors. If you have never undertaken a SWOT analysis before, SWOT stands for: Strengths, Weaknesses, Opportunities and Threats.

SWOT analysis

Any good corporate property strategy should have sight of the big issues associated with the portfolio. As you work through a portfolio SWOT analysis, you will identify strengths, weaknesses, opportunities and threats that are not only portfolio-wide, but those which are specific to a particular portfolio segment/s. If that happens, it's great news as you are starting to see the value in the segmentation process.

If the issues you face with your property portfolio vary depending on the nature of the asset, you might decide to split the SWOT apart – one for each segment. This means that the organisational response will also need to be different. The diagram below shows a simplified SWOT analysis around a commercial property portfolio segment by way of example. If done well and diligently, a good SWOT analysis can be really useful.

STRENGTHS	WEAKNESSES
Good quality investments	High exposure to retail market
Strong tenant covenants	Poor carbon performance
Sub-division to smaller units	Changing trading conditions, markets and supply chains
Redevelopment marriage value	Government regulation of local authority finance
OPPORTUNITIES	THREATS

SWOT analysis example for a commercial property portfolio segment

When you eventually have your corporate property strategy in place, you can revisit your SWOT on a sub-segment or an asset-by-asset basis as part of developing your asset management plan or delivery plan, within a detailed asset challenge process.

Risk models

One way of thinking about threats to the property portfolio is to consider the risks the portfolio is subject to, or could create. There have been a couple of attempts by local authorities over the years to create risk-based models for asset management. I am not certain they were ever as effective as they could have been, but the idea of a risk-based model has always fascinated me. The trick is to think in a completely different way about the portfolio. The starting point is not what you believe the portfolio is there to do or to create. Instead, the approach is based upon the theory the property portfolio is only there to achieve outcomes. If you can clearly define those outcomes (and they may well be organisational outcomes), then you can create a model that establishes where the property portfolio or segment can help or hinder the achievement of those outcomes, and can tell you the extent of the risk in achieving or not achieving those outcomes.

The two examples I have seen both followed a slightly different path. The first time I came across this sort of thought process was an asset management plan produced by an English District Council. I remember featuring it in a presentation in a round-up of different asset management plan approaches I gave around 2007. I came across the replacement asset management plan of that same local authority a few years later. The first thing I noticed was they had ditched the risk-based model and reverted to a more traditional approach. I do not know why that was. Maybe it didn't work as they hoped it would. Maybe there was a change in manager that decided to take asset management planning in a different direction. Maybe someone thought because nobody else was taking this approach, it was somehow the wrong thing to do. If that was the case, it's a shame. As Jodie Foster once said, 'Normal is not something to aspire to, it's something to get away from.'[7]

The second time I came across any sort of risk-based model was in 2016. It was based on a publicly available 'Logic Model' approach, whose precise origins are disputed. A logic model can often be a graphic which represents the theory of how an intervention produces its outcomes. It provides a visual means to represent the relationship between resources, into activities, and then leading to changes (or outcomes) and ultimately the 'impact' of the asset.[8] I saw its application when this particular authority's asset management plan was going through a rewrite, and they sent me a draft asking for my observations on what they were creating. I found it interesting, and it was certainly a great deal more sophisticated than the earlier, risk-based model I had seen.

The difference with the Logic Model is that it starts with assessing the impact you want to have and works backwards along a 'critical path' to consider what outcome will deliver that impact. Working backwards from the outcome, you consider what outputs would be needed to create that outcome. Finally, you identify the range of activities that will generate the required outputs. In that sense it follows a logical and consistent methodology.

By way of example, the table below is my own, simplified hypothetical recreation of the Logic Model to explain what this might look like graphically, where the aim is for property assets to be safe and available.

Impact	Outcome	Outputs	Activities
Property assets are safe for users and available for operations	Property assets are kept in good condition	Repair and maintenance minor works programmes and capital programme	Surveys and inspections
			Repairs response times
			Capital programme prioritisation
			Stakeholder surveys

The Logic Model approach need not be limited to activities and impact internally within the property function. The approach can have a much wider application. The second hypothetical example shown in the table below shows the relationship of property-related activities as part of a more strategic organisational impact, such as the area of 'healthy communities' in this case.

Impact	Outcome	Outputs	Activities
Healthy communities	Higher usage of leisure facilities, sports pitches and parks	Leisure facilities, sports pitches and parks are plentiful through an assessment of strategic need Leisure facilities, sports pitches and parks are attractive to users through capital improvements and upgrades	Surveys and inspections Repairs response Capital programme prioritisation Stakeholder surveys Leasing policy to sports club operators

Sadly, I am not certain this model ever lived up to its potential. I am not even sure if the asset management plan was adopted using this approach, but I still maintain there has to be something in this. There is a risk-based model out there somewhere waiting to be created. Maybe this discussion fascinates you enough for you to be the one inspired to create it…

Top tips

- When segmenting your property portfolio, stick to wide categories. Avoid getting bogged down in the weeds or spending too long debating (with yourself or others) the relative merits of individual assets and which segment they should or could fall into.

- When you are allocating assets to segments, if there is some doubt as to the segment allocation, place the asset into a temporary segment for later discussion.

- Review all the categories and descriptors you are using in your database, making sure there are no 'duplicate' categories in the singular and plural (for example, 'Play Area' and 'Play Areas'). Also, make sure no asset description has the word 'former' in it.

- To bring even more power to your assessment of portfolio risks, consider combining your SWOT analysis with a PESTLE analysis, which stands for: Political, Economic, Social, Technological, Legal and Environmental.

Summary

In this chapter, I introduced you to the first of my six Ps – your Portfolio. You should now have much greater clarity on what property portfolio you have, and the key segments within it.

I have shown you how the way you have categorised assets in the past may have muddled your thinking and restricted you from seeing the broad nature of your portfolio. This holds back property strategy. I also talked you through how to segment the portfolio so you have clear, broad asset categories which will serve you well in future steps. Finally, I encouraged you to undertake a portfolio SWOT analysis of your chosen asset groupings.

If you have undertaken the three steps in this chapter, you will now have a far better understanding of your property portfolio. You may even feel a sense of relief as you feel more enlightened about your property portfolio and gain a better understanding of your property portfolio than you ever have before. You will be energised for the next step, which is to apply your mind to why you have these assets, how the portfolio aligns to organisational objectives and what you expect of your portfolio going forward.

FOUR
Purpose

In the previous chapter, you built your understanding of your organisation's property portfolio and the main portfolio segments. You also made a start in identifying opportunities and risks across the portfolio, and within portfolio segments. The next step in your journey towards a corporate property strategy is to establish a clear purpose for the property portfolio. In this chapter you will develop better clarity of purpose of each of the portfolio segments, how that aligns with organisational goals and what your expectations are for each part of the portfolio.

There are three elements to the Purpose step:

1. Desire: Bringing clarity
2. Direction: Organisational alignment
3. Deliverables: Expectation criteria

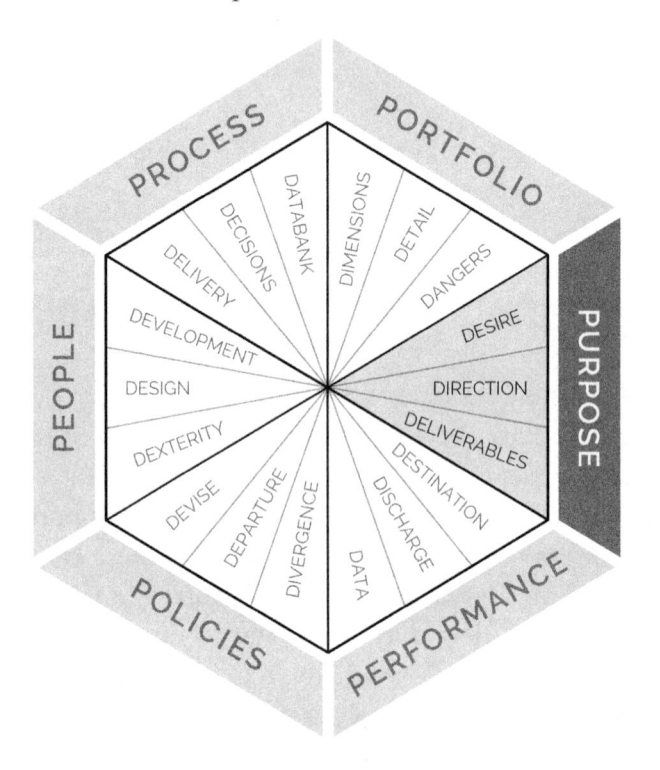

Desire: Bringing clarity

It is so important in strategic asset management to know what your high-level desires are of your property portfolio. You need to be clear on the general direction, but too often this step in the process is not thought through. It is important to understand what your property portfolio needs to deliver, and why you need to deliver it. Strategic asset management is a simple process of supply and demand. This relies on you knowing what the organisational demand is for property assets, which is driven by their purpose. You also need to know what those property assets need to look and behave like to be effective and deliver the outcomes you seek to achieve. If you can establish that, you are a great deal further ahead with asset management than many. While that may sound simple in theory, it is not always as simple in practice.

Supply Demand model

The supply/demand tension as the root of asset management was a realisation I came to when I was working in local government in the early days of asset management around 2001. It was a bit of a 'eureka' moment for me.

That train of thought led me to experiment in my approach to asset management planning. In those days, asset management planning was a property discipline in its infancy. In fact, to many it was not yet a discipline at all, it was just a bunch of people swanning around not doing proper work. Many in the property team (including some senior managers) hadn't the first clue what I and others were doing. That was frustrating at times, but it also was liberating. There was no rulebook to follow. Some struggle in that kind of environment. Others flourish.

I flourished. I found there was freedom to play around with ideas, experiment, innovate, make mistakes. Some things worked, some things didn't. One idea which I would have liked to see work, but didn't, was finding a way to get some value from this obvious supply/demand tension. I devised a 'supply demand model', similar to the diagram below. My model was founded on the premise that most services probably do not have the property assets they need. They may be the wrong size, the incorrect configuration, they may be too hot or too cold, they may be too expensive or they may simply be in the wrong place for the customers and communities they serve. Maybe they are no longer needed at all. All those are relevant aspects any asset manager and service manager should at some point consider.

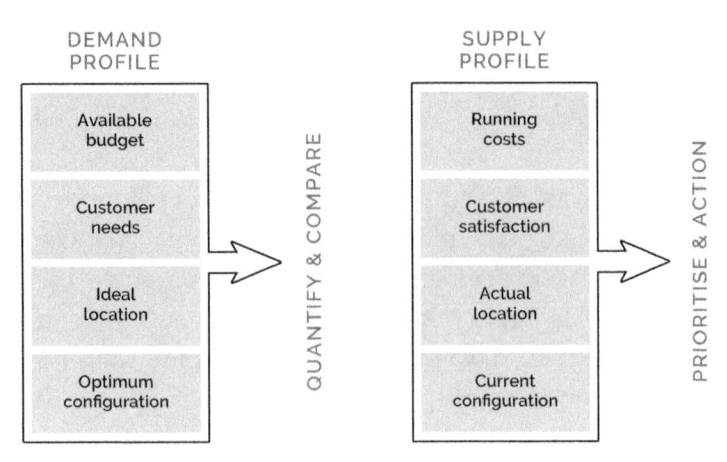

DEMAND PROFILE		SUPPLY PROFILE	
Available budget		Running costs	
Customer needs	QUANTIFY & COMPARE	Customer satisfaction	PRIORITISE & ACTION
Ideal location		Actual location	
Optimum configuration		Current configuration	

Supply demand model

The difference with the supply demand model is the starting point. The starting point is not the assets currently in use, but a blank sheet of paper. That blank sheet of paper can be more valuable than you might think at first. It is rooted in the Buddhist theory of what is termed 'beginner's mind' or 'shoshin'.[9] The process requires that the service manager approach the process with an open mind and imagine that their current service, and its associated property assets, do not exist.

The first stage of the model is to design the service from the bottom up to decide what aspects of their service needs property assets, and then (assuming some property assets are needed), what those assets might ideally look like and where they would need to be. I have called this the 'asset demand profile'. A head of service once said to me,

> 'This was the main model I used when trying to engage service managers who could not visualise anything other than their existing portfolio. It was a great tool to free them from the constraints of what they already had to work with and to dream of what they could have.'

This supply demand approach lifts service managers from the constraints of their existing operational portfolio. It also allows the organisation to contemplate zero-based budgeting, which in turn can often lead to budget savings and re-alignment.

The second stage of the model is to map the assets the service actually has – what I call the 'asset supply profile'. Comparing this with the ideal service property portfolio (the 'asset demand profile') identifies gaps where the current portfolio for that service is falling short, is not good enough, is too expensive or is in the wrong place or the wrong configuration. This gives you some actionable targets to move the service portfolio from where you are now (generally underperforming in some aspect) to where you need to be (as best you can, the ideal portfolio for that service).

Some years later, I was doing research into different approaches to asset management plans by local authorities while preparing a presentation. I came across the asset management plan of a local authority in the Midlands that contained a supply demand model. It looked just like the one I had produced and used a few years earlier. I got the opportunity to speak with the author of that particular asset management plan as part of the research for this book. What was interesting was the challenges they had experienced in embedding the approach, which mirrored my experience. They said:

> 'For those not regularly dealing with property, the notion of a blank sheet or clean starting position can seem like a theoretical exercise, so as part of the collaboration service, managers need to appreciate the outcomes that can be delivered.'

The lesson is that while concepts, theories and ideas are great, not everyone will get it. In this case, service managers had struggled with the 'blank sheet of paper' principle. When service managers talked about their needs for property assets, they couldn't shake from their heads the property assets they were already using or occupying. They may have been good at managing and delivering their service, but they were not necessarily suited to service design. They struggled with the 'beginner's mind' approach. What the supply/demand tension approach needs is engagement with people who have a service design mindset. They are great people if you can find them. They will make your life a great deal easier.

One service area where I have seen it work is a Council Youth Service. They got the concept straight away. They recognised that they didn't actually need physical and dedicated youth centres that stood empty for most of the day. All they needed was space for youth activities, and it didn't need to be a council-run youth centre. In fact, in some respects, the constraints of the typical youth centre restricted the range of activities the service could make available.

Engagement at service level is only part of determining asset purpose. There also needs to be higher level engagement with directors, board members, elected officials (mayor, PPC, etc) or cabinet members – depending on how your organisation is governed and who the key decision-makers and policy-shapers are.

I talked earlier in this book about the need to understand personal motivations of stakeholders, whether that is local issues, global issues or anything in between. This is where preparatory work becomes so valuable. Whether engaging with service managers or decision-makers, you need to tap into their motivations. Without doing that, you may struggle to get the engagement you need. If you can help service managers understand the benefits to themselves and to provide assurance that positive change is possible, then they will engage. And if they engage, they will own the strategy with you, greatly improving the odds of successful implementation and of the organisation 'living' the strategy.

Clarifying the purpose of your segments

In the previous chapter I took you through a process of segmenting the property portfolio. How many segments (and even sub-segments) you have will be dictated by the nature and characteristics of your portfolio. You now need to articulate a clear asset purpose for each segment of the property portfolio. A great deal of thinking will have been done during the segmentation process, but it will need revisiting. You have allocated every asset to a segment. If you followed the top tips at the end of that chapter you may have a temporary portfolio segment, which you are not sure what to do with. Your next task is to review all the portfolio segments, working through each in turn. Develop a brief and clear statement as to the purpose of each. In other words, 'What is the portfolio segment there to do?' It might be around supporting local communities or business or it might be about generating income. These are just examples, but each segment should end up with that clear statement, because a clear statement provides space and focus for discussion.

Once you have your segment statements, share them with others. Circulate it to colleagues, both within the property team and elsewhere. Share it with service managers, directors and relevant portfolio holders. Follow this up with a facilitated workshop. Get all interested parties in the room to talk through each aspect of what you have drafted. Make sure you are clear on the different motivations of those in the room. Let this help shape the narrative for the session. Find out what people agree with and what people disagree with. Your aim is to not leave that room until you are clear on the purpose of each segment of your property portfolio. You may well find disagreements that need to be resolved.

Where you get disagreements on what a particular portfolio segment's purpose is, do not get disheartened. Most of all, do not allow disagreement to undermine this essential step. Use disagreements as an opportunity to resolve issues and come away with clarity. You may well find disagreements on segment purpose begin to highlight you do not yet have the segments quite right. Perhaps there are actually two or more separate segments with different purposes within what you thought was a single segment. Your facilitated discussion can draw this out. Believe me, you will feel empowered by the process.

CASE STUDY: ASSET PURPOSE

I recently attended a corporate asset group of a local authority client and our conversation highlighted the issue of misalignment of purpose. One of the council's directors reported that the council's farms estate was performing really well. Income was up and was performing among the best in the country.

In response, one of the elected members made the comment they believed the farms estate was not held for financial return, but to help support new tenant farmers into the industry. Someone else in the meeting felt the real benefit of having a farms estate was to be able to promote biodiversity, access to the countryside and promote the issue of food miles. This is a classic, and far from unique, situation which I often observe. That single meeting had highlighted a complete misalignment of purpose for the council's farms estate. It showed a lack of previous discussion and openness about why the council had a farms estate.

The impact of misalignment, of course, is that everyone has a different perspective on what good performance looks like. Depending on how well the farms estate is doing in those three examples of performance, someone is likely to be disappointed. The officers managing that part of the estate are perhaps going to receive criticism whatever they do, which is a no-win situation for the asset manager.

The action point in this example is to generate a wider discussion and reach consensus so both officers and elected members can agree on what the purpose of those properties is and manage performance accordingly.

PURPOSE

The diagram below is a simplified example of how you might want to think about mapping your portfolio segments and the purpose of each. Please do not use it as a starting point; that is not my purpose in including it. This simple example is here to demonstrate a suggested approach, nothing more.

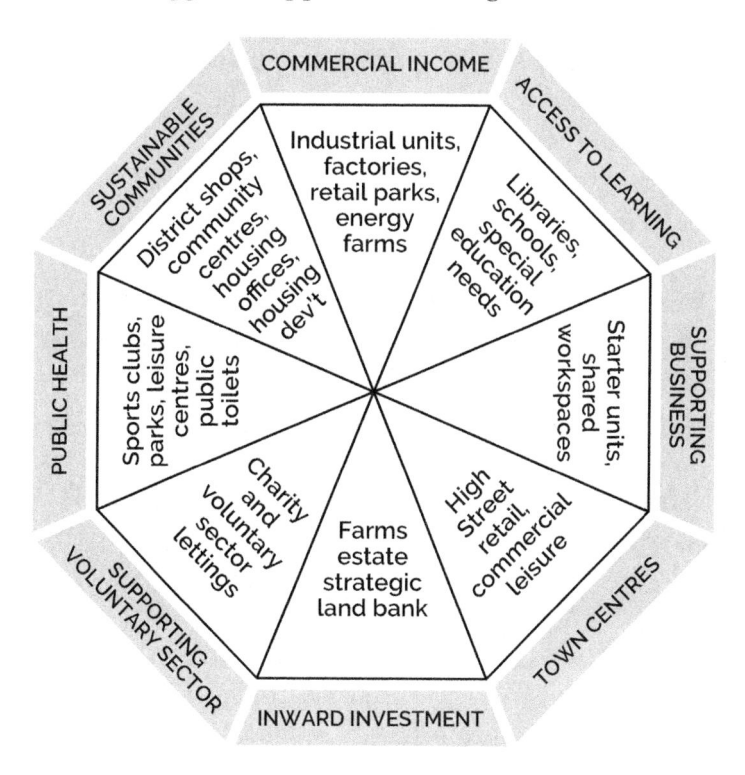

Mapping your portfolio segments example

Assume you work for a local authority that has assets leased out to GP surgeries. Which segment should these sit in on the diagram above? Clearly, the answer is not the nature of the use, but the reason you have

75

those assets. You may decide these are health related and fit nicely into the 'public health' segment. After discussion though, you may conclude that in fact they are held primarily for securing rental income, in which case they may fit better into the 'commercial income' segment. That is the sort of discussion needed on every part of your property portfolio. It is especially important when you begin to examine property performance in Chapter 5. The performance expectations of those GP surgeries could be distinctly different, depending on which of those segments you agree they should be in.

You need to discuss with stakeholders and reach agreement. Aim to create a segment purpose diagram along the lines of the simplified example in the diagram above. You will hopefully reach a consensus across the organisation. You will have prompted discussions that quite possibly have not taken place before. The clarity this will bring will be hugely valuable.

Direction: Organisational alignment

Strategy without purpose is pointless. With clarity of purpose, you can begin to seek some alignment of the property portfolio with your organisational goals or objectives. In the preparation for embarking on the 6 Ps journey as set out in Chapter 2, I tasked you with reading and digesting all the current (and draft) organisational and service strategies and policies your organisation has in place, and which are relevant to your property strategy development. This is where what you learned from those documents comes into use.

If you followed my recommended approach, you should now have a schedule of the key property implications arising out of those documents. You will also have a greater and more robust understanding of what your organisation is seeking to achieve, and a more detailed understanding of each service and their goals. From that work, you should have at hand a schedule of the principal areas where either a) property assets will be a fundamental part of achieving an aspiration, or b) where strategic initiatives are going to impact on the property portfolio. This will be at the heart of your corporate property strategy.

Armed with this information, you can now begin to align each main portfolio segment with a key organisational or service objective. A grid matrix works well. List the main property groups down the left-hand side of your grid and create a column for each key organisational or service objective across the top of your grid. The diagram below provides an example you can base this on. For the purposes of the diagram, I have adopted the segment purposes I used in the previous diagram as my portfolio segments. This is simply to demonstrate the approach and may not be a fair representation of your portfolio segments. For this example, it matters not whether you agree with where the ticks are. It is just a simple example.

Council Plan Objectives / Portfolio Segments	Vibrant & Sustainable Economy	Meeting Housing Needs	Strong, Active & Healthy Communities	Clean & Sustainable Borough	Efficient & Effective Council	Fair & Inclusive Society	Empowering & Caring
Access to Learning	✓					✓	✓
Supporting Business	✓						
Town Centres	✓	✓	✓	✓		✓	
Inward Investment	✓	✓		✓	✓		
Supporting Voluntary Sector	✓		✓				✓
Public Health		✓	✓	✓		✓	✓
Sustainable Communities		✓	✓	✓		✓	✓
Commercial Income	✓				✓		

Organisational objectives matrix

Work your way through the grid. It doesn't matter whether you work from top to bottom or from side to side. Do whatever you feel comfortable with. The important thing is to consider where each asset segment has the opportunity to impact on each of the organisational or service goals. You might start simply with a series of ticks, but I recommend you move beyond that to describe the links. Try to be strict with yourself and avoid ticking every box in every column and row as this will not help you. The purpose of this is to identify the main linkages by differentiating which assets support primarily which objectives. Where you are not sure, mark the grid cell accordingly. You don't have to get this perfect the first time around, it may take a number of attempts.

Some organisational objectives will span all or a number of property portfolio segments. It is important to recognise where those exist and not lose sight of them during this process. You should have identified if these exist when you went through your preparation described in Chapter 2. For example, any objectives around efficient use of resources (which will presumably include property assets) or perhaps achieving net zero carbon as part of a climate change or carbon management strategy would both be good examples of such pan-organisational objectives.

Once you are happy with where you are, share it with colleagues. Seek validation. Seek criticism. Make it clear this is your personal view and you need the views of others so you can reach a consensus. When you have received feedback, you will see that there is broad agreement in many of the areas. You now have two fresh tasks. The first is to revisit the areas where you appear to have agreement. The second is to seek a consensus on the areas where there is disagreement or conflicting feedback. They are both equally important.

You might at this stage be wondering why you would revisit what people think on areas where there appears to be agreement. The reason is something called 'group think'. This is the tendency for people to agree with what others have said, perhaps because they feel the other person has better knowledge, or even because of the status of that individual in the organisation. I recommend you work through the areas of agreement in a workshop environment and play devil's advocate. Imagine you are preparing for something like an Oxford Union debate, with the task of disagreeing with the assertions inferred by the areas of consensus. What arguments are there for saying these areas of consensus are incorrect? As you are doing this, you may well hit a gem of an idea that challenges accepted thinking. If so, make a note of it.

For example, if your organisation has industrial properties in its portfolio, you might have initially said they align with the organisational objective on economic regeneration. When others saw your view, they may have agreed with it. They may have done so because they don't really know anything about the industrial portfolio and presume you have greater knowledge. After all, they see you as the property 'expert'. When you revisit that tick – even where there is consensus – you need to challenge your perceptions and views. Does the industrial portfolio really support economic regeneration? How does it do that? Are these properties ultimately now for financial return only? That is the sort of challenge you need to bring to yourself and to others. Perhaps the industrial units were originally constructed fifteen years ago to create business space as part of an economic regeneration activity. Are they still contributing to that original objective, or have they moved into being a purely financial transaction based on rental income levels?

One way to bring clarity on that is to consider the means by which performance of the assets is broadly judged, which I will discuss further in Chapter 5. Is the asset manager judged principally on rental income and vacant space, or on the number of new businesses supported and jobs created?

Your second task is to get all interested parties together for another facilitated workshop session. Start by working through each of the areas where there is no consensus. Let everyone have their view. Seek to understand the different perspectives. Do not leave that room until there is agreement and you have a consensus.

Deliverables: Expectation criteria

Strategy development can be more important than the strategy itself. When you have clarity on the purpose of each segment of the portfolio, and the alignment with organisational objectives and priorities, you can develop the deliverables. These are the things you want each portfolio segment to deliver for you. This will vary from asset type to asset type, and may even vary between local authorities. It depends on the particular issues and challenges your organisation faces, and what social or community interventions your organisation is focused on. Without completing this step, you will struggle to make adequate headway into the asset performance issues we will discuss in the next chapter.

CASE STUDY: CLARITY OF ASSET PURPOSE

When I was a valuer working at Bristol City Council, one of the properties I was asked to manage was a small industrial estate located in a suburb of the city. It was a terrace of small starter units. The estate had been built by the council a few years previous to my involvement, with the sole purpose of providing business space to new small businesses. The original concept was great. Small units, let out on 'easy in, easy out' terms. The concept was a place for small businesses to establish themselves, grow and move on to bigger premises.

Somehow, between that decision to build the estate and me being asked to manage it, the estate had lost its original purpose. Nobody quite knew when that happened, but it had and there was little going back. Low demand resulted in high void rates. This triggered a historic change in estate management. I inherited multiple units let to the same tenant. Some units were let to large, established firms.

The original purpose of the estate had been lost along the way. It had never been revisited to see if its original purpose was still valid, or whether the market needed this type of space.

List each of your portfolio segments as a series of headings. Under each heading, start setting out what you believe to be the main deliverables for that portfolio segment. In the previous part of this chapter, I encouraged you to gather together senior decision-makers and service managers to agree the purpose of each segment and alignment with organisational and service objectives. Now you need to dig deeper.

Facilitate another workshop to establish what people believe should be the main deliverables for each segment. Property assets held for their financial return may seem fairly straightforward at first glance, but there are still decisions to be made. The main deliverable could be the revenue generated, or it could be capital growth or yield. If it is the yield, which sort of yield is important to you? If you are a property valuer or investment valuer, you will know exactly what I mean by that. It is important to know, as you will need that decision when you begin to build your performance framework which I talk about in Chapter 5.

If the segments that are driven by financial deliverables are not as straightforward as you might have thought, I am not surprised. When you turn to non-financial deliverables, things will get ever more complex. I could quite possibly devote a whole book to discussing the possible range of non-financial outcomes. There is simply not the space here to do that. If you have worked in the public sector for a while, you will know exactly why I say that. What I can help with are some starter questions for you to use in your facilitated workshop. These might include:

- If the deliverable is not about money, is it about economic outcomes or more social outcomes?

- What are the specific deliverables you are aiming for by holding these property assets? Perhaps it is things like access to learning, health and wellbeing, regeneration, transport, reducing crime, public health, public safety or any number of other outcomes. Some of these outcomes will be linked to statutory duties and others to non-statutory (or 'discretionary') services.

- Who occupies and uses these assets? Are they commercial organisations or organisations that operate with a social purpose? Does this affect your expectations on deliverables?

- What would the impact be if that portfolio segment was not there? Who would notice? How would they notice? Who, or what, would be impacted most?

If you can work through those questions, you will start to identify the key deliverables for each of the portfolio segments.

Top tips

- Ask your service managers to list what they regard as their top and bottom three properties, and why. This will tell you a lot about their needs and priorities.

- When segmenting the portfolio, agree the principles for segmentation in advance. An agreed rationale and principles make it harder for later disagreement.

- When aligning segment purpose to organisational objectives, it may help during the first attempt to split this into 'significant' and 'minor' contribution.

- When developing segment purpose, ask yourself who benefits the most when the portfolio segment is performing as it should, and who is negatively impacted if the portfolio segment is not performing as it should.

Summary

In this chapter we have built on what we did in Chapter 3 and started to take the knowledge of your portfolio to another level. You have developed a fuller understanding of the purpose and direction for each portfolio segment and drilled even deeper to identify the expectation criteria of each of those portfolio segments. You have pushed yourself and others into a greater understanding of each portfolio segment, and why you have it. If you have been thorough and you have engaged well with others through the process, you should have more clarity around your property portfolio than you ever thought possible.

This will prepare you well for the next chapter, where we build upon those expectation criteria and deliverables and start to develop a performance framework which will tell you what performance you should be targeting for each portfolio segment, how that compares to current performance, and how to tackle the performance gaps.

FIVE
Performance

In the Sir Arthur Conan Doyle short story, 'A Scandal in Bohemia', there is a scene where Sherlock Holmes has just finished reading a letter to Watson.[10] Watson asks Holmes what the letter means, to which Holmes issues the perfect reply: 'It is a capital mistake to theorise before one has data. Insensibly one begins to twist facts to suit theories, instead of theories to suit facts.'

If ever there was a statement that sums up what is often the approach to property performance management, and indeed the development of business cases, in local government, that is it. In this chapter you will discover a new, better way to look at property performance management. The importance of this aspect of developing your corporate property strategy cannot be underestimated. It is the third of the 'push' elements. Remember, you are pushing yourself and the organisation into a critical appraisal of what you want your property portfolio to look like, and to be.

There are three elements to the Performance step:

1. Destination: Setting performance areas
2. Discharge: Establishing current performance
3. Data: Performance and data gaps

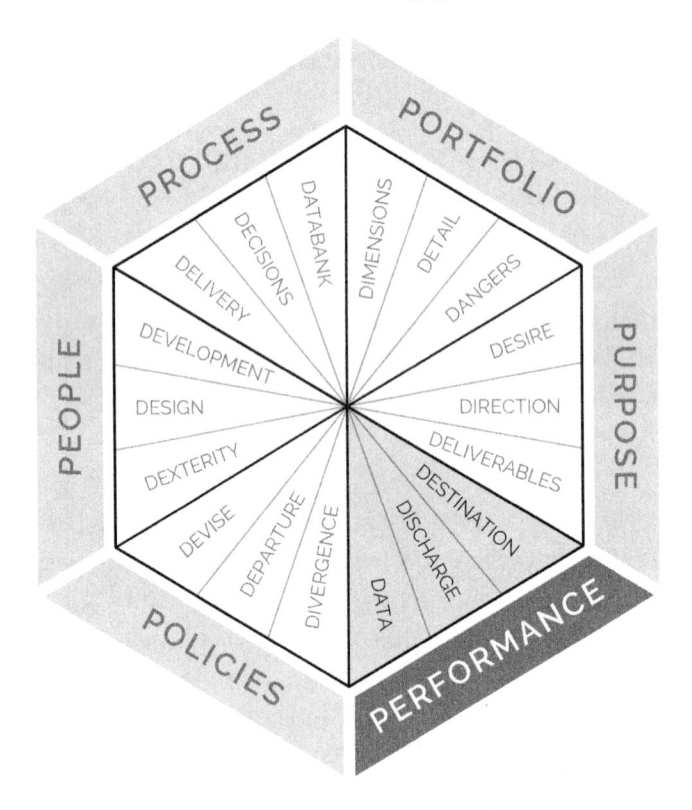

Destination: Setting performance areas

Many approach the area of property asset performance through the lens of a property professional. It is understandable. That is how people are often conditioned to think and act. What that lens looks like depends on which specific property discipline people come from but most property professionals have this in common: they like to measure physical things that they can easily count. Too often, asset performance starts and finishes with measuring what is already being measured or what is easy to measure. Too few link performance to asset purpose.

The challenge is to move beyond the typical approach and adopt a performance management framework that measures what is important to measure. Common performance areas such as property condition, running costs, space utilisation, income, carbon impact, energy performance, etc, have their place and may have relevance across much of the portfolio. It may be that for some parts of the property portfolio, these performance areas are less important than economic or social measures, particularly where assets are held in supporting the local economy or delivering community outcomes. These performance metrics are often harder to nail down.

You have to work out your own direction on this. Look beyond the traditional property performance metric and consider areas along the lines of utilisation of community facilities, re-occupancy of social care properties, satisfaction with teaching environments or maybe jobs created or supported. The potential list is endless.

Developing performance measures

It is important your performance measures distinguish good performance from bad performance. This may sound obvious, but many people fall into this trap. An example is one of the national performance measures devised for the National Property Performance Management Initiative a few years ago. One performance measure captured what each organisation had spent on property maintenance, so this could be compared between organisations and also tracked internally over time. Don't get me wrong, this is good to know, but in isolation it tells you little. Let's say you have that figure for your organisation: would you regard your performance as being good the more you spend, or the less you spend? On its own as a strategic performance measure, simply knowing what you spend on maintenance is pretty useless. It doesn't contribute to performance improvement.

If, however, you combine that measure with the condition of the portfolio, you have a more powerful measure. You know what you are spending in relation to what the need is. If you compare that to others in a benchmarking exercise, you would soon see how your performance compares. You will also begin to form a picture of whether, on your current spend trajectory, the condition of your properties is likely to be improving or deteriorating. I cannot tell you what the right things are for you to measure and manage, but there are three critical factors to consider when you do. These are shown in the diagram below.

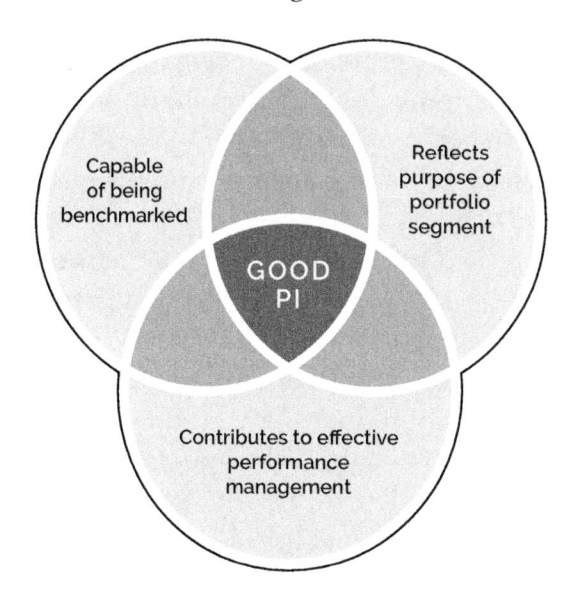

Good Performance Indicator test

What to measure

Whichever performance measures you choose, they should be divided into two groups: those areas of performance important on a whole portfolio basis and those which relate to specific portfolio segments. Both are important to have an effective and relevant performance framework. That's why tackling the segmentation of the property portfolio is so important.

Whole portfolio measures should be high-level and strategic. They might relate to areas of use you might typically see included in a State of the Estate report, such as that produced annually by the cabinet office. They are higher level areas of performance across the whole property portfolio, both operational and commercial. They provide a picture of the overall strategic direction when measured year to year. They show improvement or deterioration at a macro-level.

At the macro-level, areas of performance might include property condition, costs, occupancy rates, environmental performance or fitness for performance. Please do not take those examples as definitive or necessarily appropriate for you and your portfolio. They are examples only. As background reading, you might want to review the new International Building Operation Standard published by the RICS.[11] This talks about five pillars of performance: Compliant, Functional, Economic, Sustainable and Performing.

Segment performance measures should not be on a whole portfolio basis, but relate to specific portfolio segments. As I don't know what your portfolio segments will be, I cannot tell you what these segment performance areas should be, but they need to relate to important areas of performance for each segment. Some segments may have similar performance areas.

The performance areas that you have decided are important on a whole portfolio basis may also be important at a portfolio segment level. There is nothing wrong with that.

Some segments, though, will have performance areas specific to them. As an example, if you have a commercial or investment portfolio, financial performance may be the primary performance area. When it comes to deciding performance measures, these will relate to that purpose. If you hold a commercial portfolio, it may be for reasons other than its financial performance, or for reasons alongside its financial performance. In that case, you would want to adopt performance measures that relate to all those performance areas. For example, for you, that segment might be more about the number of jobs created or retained, or the number of businesses supported than about financial performance. In some cases, you may find property performance measures blending with service performance measures. That is quite normal. That's why creating a corporate property strategy is an organisational activity, and not a property activity.

You should work through each portfolio segment and make a judgement about what things are important to that segment, why it is important and to what extent it is important. You may need to challenge yourself, colleagues and elected members to expose the heart of performance for each portfolio segment. This can be a cathartic experience if you dive deeply into it in a facilitated workshop environment. Think about the council farms case study in the previous chapter. In that example, if you had clarity of purpose, you would have clarity of expectations. If you had clarity of expectations, you would be able to develop clear performance measures. Performance measures for county farms could range from absolute financial return, to yield on capital, to capital growth, to the number of tenant entrants, to the number of tenants supported, to levels of biodiversity, to food mile reductions, land quality and all manner of other possible measures.

Performance targets

Performance targets you adopt will depend on many variables, including your current level of performance, ambitions, availability of resources and overall relative priorities. Targets may vary between assets in the same segment. Taking asset condition as an example, assets in 24/7 use, such as residential care settings, may need a higher performance target than other frontline facilities. After all, it is someone's home and people living there may be vulnerable or need a higher-quality environment.

People often ask me whether performance targets and performance standards are the same thing. The answer is, not necessarily. Targets are something you are aiming for. Standards are generally the minimum levels you seek to maintain. If you have set a performance standard such as a minimum condition standard for a certain portfolio segment and you have yet to attain that standard, it is effectively a performance target. Once a performance standard is achieved, you may then consider setting a target that exceeds that standard.

You do not need to focus in too much detail on performance targets for your corporate property strategy. At this stage, it should be enough to keep to high-level targets, especially where data is incomplete or unreliable. Whatever performance targets you go for should be chosen because they relate to the first Ps of my 6 Ps methodology. This means your performance targets are your own and not someone else's. This is one reason why internal benchmarking is often more valuable than external benchmarking. Performance targets for the property portfolio should be based on well-defined indicators lacking ambiguity. They should be challenging, but achievable. That is not an easy path to follow, and you will find a great deal of iteration is needed.

Performance culture

Different organisations have different performance management cultures. Some encourage and some discourage dashboards of performance indicators. If yours is the latter, you may need to work hard to gain support for more (or better) performance measurement.

The cost of collecting performance data and undertaking performance analysis can be significant. Some spend years trying to persuade colleagues that condition data is essential to properly understand the performance of the property portfolio, often being greeted with an attitude that lack of money to maintain buildings makes condition measurement pointless. I contend the opposite to be the case. Insufficient money to maintain your portfolio means every pound you spend must be spent wisely. Knowledge of the relative condition of your property assets then becomes more, not less, important. Lack of condition data can also lead to a reactive maintenance culture, with smaller planned maintenance programmes and a desire to build shiny new buildings rather than spending on the basics.

Organisational culture and availability of time and resources means developing a property performance framework may take many years to achieve. Targets (particularly milestone targets) are important both in helping to identify the scale of the challenge and in securing resources.

Discharge: Establishing current performance

Understanding yourself is a platform for success. The value you get from measuring current performance is dictated by the effort you put into establishing target performance. If you don't throw yourself into getting target performance right, then measuring current performance will bring you far fewer benefits. If you have the wrong targets then you are looking at the wrong baseline, so when you move to the task of closing performance gaps, you are closing the wrong gaps and identifying the wrong missing data.

If you are at a point where you have some clarity on your property performance targets, you will have come a lot further than many ever do. It may not be perfect. You will want to revisit it.

If you have done a thorough job on target performance, you will have identified areas of performance you have not previously measured. That means for some of your adopted performance measures, you may have no available data on current performance. You have no baseline. If you have no baseline, you may not yet have a complete set of targets, as you may not yet know what challenges you face and performance gaps you need to close.

Benchmarking

Benchmarking does not have to mean trawling the country for like organisations that want to measure what you measure. Even where organisations have many similarities, the portfolios, circumstances or priorities are rarely ever the same. Finding someone that defines performance and measures it the same as you can be a challenge, and may not always be that valuable. While external performance benchmarking can have its place, a mistake many make is selecting performance measures all participants know they can benchmark. Performance measurement based on what other people collect is no basis for performance management. This can lead you down a dark and fruitless road. Believe me, I have been there.

CASE STUDY: PERFORMANCE INDICATOR DEFINITION

I spent many years attending meetings of the Core Cities Asset Strategy Group, the purpose of which was to benchmark property performance. We started, as many do, by sharing what we already knew about the performance of our portfolios. Where we found common ground on performance areas, we spent a great deal of time defining the performance measure to make sure all eight (as they were then) Core City authorities were collecting the data in exactly the same way, so a meaningful comparison could be made.

We discovered that while we could arrive at a robust performance measurement definition, there was not a single definition that matched enough of the contributors and the way they collected data. We each had to change how we collected and analysed data.

After several years of meetings and a great deal of effort and determination, the end result was a group which certainly compared performance data, but every performance report was filled with caveats explaining why the data did not precisely compare.

There is often more merit in internal benchmarking. This shows year-on-year performance change, and also shows performance differences between similar types of assets. When you benchmark internally, the monitoring of performance change is within your control and follows your actions and your investment in time or money. You have total freedom to define performance in a specific way valuable to you.

Whatever benchmarking you undertake, it is important that you compare data on a like-for-like basis. That is always more challenging with external benchmarking, as you have no control over data sources, quality or analysis provided by others. Where you benchmark internally, meaningful like-for-like comparisons become much more achievable. For example, if you dispose of some assets between data measurement points, you might find your maintenance backlog has fallen. This may not be down to you investing more money in priority areas, it might simply be that the backlog associated with the assets you no longer own are no longer included in the backlog calculation. Where you find yourself in such a situation, you may need to manipulate historic data to provide you with a more meaningful comparison of performance, or perhaps report your measure on two different bases.

Perverse incentive

You may have heard the term 'perverse incentive'. It is a trap you need to be alert to when setting performance targets and in performance reporting. A perverse incentive is an incentive with an unintended and undesirable result that is contrary to the intentions of its designers. In this context, your performance measures and targets operate as the incentive (at least, you hope they will). Your challenge is to think deeply how any measure you devise could change behaviour or result in outcomes that are not desirable.

Perverse incentive is sometimes referred to as the 'cobra effect', a term coined by economist, Horst Siebert.[12] He relates how, during the period of imperial rule in India, the British government were apparently so concerned about the number of cobras in the city of Delhi that they offered a reward for every dead cobra. That sounded like a great plan to everybody, I am sure. Initially, it was successful in reducing cobra numbers, but it created a perverse incentive. The people of Delhi were enterprising. Some realised they could begin to breed cobras in captivity, kill them and claim the reward. The British government eventually found out and scrapped the reward scheme. That resulted in captive, and now worthless, cobras being released into the wild. By the end of the programme, the number of cobras in Delhi had increased.

Data: Performance and data gaps

We now move on to a critical step in developing your property performance framework, identifying the performance gaps and data gaps. Performance gaps will exist and can be assessed where you already have a performance baseline and performance targets. Data gaps exist where you have identified a key area of performance, but you have no current baseline to work from.

The first of those, in one sense, is the easiest. You know what level of performance you are seeking. You have the existing data. With these two pieces of information, you can express the performance gap. Closing that performance gap will be a key aspiration for you in your corporate property strategy. Where data has not previously been used in a performance management framework, some time may be needed to make sure you are able to have the data presented in a form that serves your specific purpose. For example, if you have a commercial property segment to your portfolio, data on rent arrears should be available somewhere in the finance system, but it may need some work to get it into the form you need or to isolate data for the specific segment you are interested in.

The second area is not so much difficult as time-consuming and potentially costly. If you have data gaps, the extent to which it is time-consuming and costly will depend on what the gaps relate to and how extensive they are. For example, if the condition of the property assets is important, then having up-to-date condition data from regular surveys, inspections or other sources will be invaluable. If survey data is a number of years old, then it is no longer current. This is a data gap and must be tackled. As one head of service once recounted to me,

> 'When I arrived at one organisation, it used indices to inflate [backlog repair] costs, but this did not take account of maintenance or capital works undertaken. This meant the data became meaningless, especially as it was used over many years to avoid the cost of renewing condition assessments.'

Depending on the extent of the survey backlog, this is a task that will need time and money. You may need to procure a full condition survey programme across all, or at least major parts of, the property portfolio. If you are sourcing this externally, it will take time to procure, for the contractor to mobilise and to undertake the surveys and to provide you with the survey reports. You need to be clear what survey data you want and how you want it presented back to you so it will be meaningful as part of your performance framework.

A note of caution at this point. Make sure that you are clear during the commissioning stage (internal or external) on what data you want, what you intend to use it for and how you want the data presented back to you. If you do not do this, you could well get data back that is of limited use without serious manipulation. This could be time-consuming and result in delays to implementation of performance improvement programmes. If you have to go back to the surveyors to ask them to present the data differently, it might cost you money, as well as time.

If the performance gap you have is around the suitability of the assets for occupiers and users, it can take many months devising the system you are going to use to build that information. If you have targets around socio-economic areas of performance, this may take even longer.

As with all aspects of this 6 Ps methodology, it is not necessary to divert away at this stage and start procuring anyone or mobilising your own people to start collecting data. That can come later. At this stage, it is enough to identify the performance and data gaps to be included within your corporate property strategy. If you feel you have the ability (and more importantly, the resource) to set up a separate project team to start collecting missing data, that might give you a head-start on your asset management plan when that time comes. Avoid striving for absolute perfection at this stage, as you may find this results in you achieving nothing.

Data quality

The better the quality of your data, the better your performance management framework. Whether you are seeking to maintain or improve performance levels, there are six key data questions that need to be asked, as set out in the diagram below.

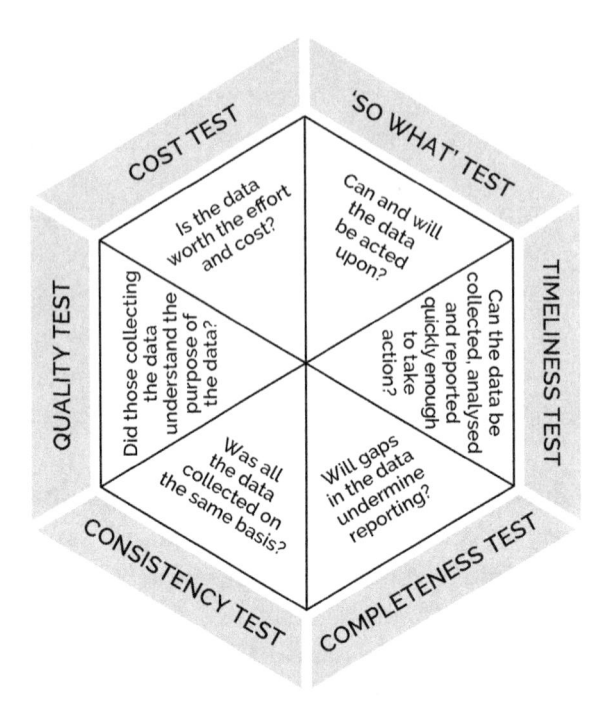

'Good data' test

- **Cost test**: Is the data worth the effort and cost?
- **'So what' test**: Can and will the data be acted upon?
- **Timeliness test**: Can the data be collected, analysed and reported quickly enough to take action?
- **Completeness test**: Will gaps in the data undermine reporting?
- **Consistency test**: Was all the data collected on the same basis?
- **Quality test**: Did those collecting the data understand the purpose of the data?

Whenever you are considering which data to collect for use in your performance management framework, keep these questions close at hand. You may find they save you a great deal of time and help you focus on prioritising data collection.

Performance reporting

Once the performance areas and targets have been mapped (both strategic and by portfolio segment), your mind should turn to how you will report performance change. Some performance improvement journeys will take longer than others, simply because some things take longer to change or turn around. Your performance reporting should take place at intervals appropriate to the performance journey you have mapped out through your target setting.

If property condition is an important performance area for you and you have decided it is something that should be reported, what exactly will you report? It could be the state of repair (repair grading), or the backlog maintenance or something else entirely. It might be a measure around the remaining physical or economic life. It may be all of those combined into a performance dashboard (which some people might call a 'balanced scorecard').

The same goes for areas such as financial performance on the commercial parts of your portfolio, where income levels, occupancy rates, return on investment, tenant debt or capital growth may be relevant. If commercial space is supporting local small businesses, there may be additional measures that could be included. Again, it is about creating the right performance dashboard. All measures should relate to the relevant performance area, should tell you what you need to know and help you on your improvement journey.

I will give you an example. With property condition, one measure might be the repair spend necessary to bring the asset to the required condition. If this measure is a portfolio measure and your interest is in showing how this figure is changing over time for the whole property portfolio, or even by portfolio segment, a single data set around condition might be adequate. If, on the other hand, you are using the measure on an asset-by-asset basis to show respective condition between assets and between portfolio segments, it is unlikely you will be seeking to express this as an absolute amount for each asset or segment. Assets and segments will be of different sizes and that would make comparison next to useless. You need another data set. In this case, it might be building floor area. The result is a single performance measure using two data sets.

Data analysis will inevitably involve some element of data manipulation. That may well involve drawing data together from multiple sources, so it is imperative there is an audit trail of how data was compiled. As you go through the data analysis and manipulation process, you may convince yourself that you will remember what you did. You won't. If you do not create a data audit trail that commits the process you went through to paper, next time you come to perform the same task you will do it slightly differently or in a different sequence. You won't realise it at the time, but when you come to compare this year's data with last year's data, the difference between the years might not actually be a change in performance. It might be down to a change in the sequence or methodology used to arrive at the reported figures. I cannot stress how important this audit trail is.

Top tips

- Measuring and managing asset performance is not always about performance improvement. It can legitimately focus on maintaining a status quo or even managing a performance decline.

- Make sure all building changes that alter floor areas have been taken into account in the property database or performance system, as lack of good, current base data is one reason why some key performance measures are either inaccurate or not utilised.

- Focus on outcomes and performance areas before setting targets or you may waste time and energy.

Summary

In this chapter, I have taken you through the process of building your property performance framework. You will have identified your target performance – or identified future tasks to do so. You will have assessed current performance against the known target performance. You will have identified performance and data gaps and identified associated actions.

Some targets may be interim as you develop your thinking and performance management framework. Some targets may be challenging to agree on because of the political or management culture but you have to work your way through this.

SIX
Policies

You have now completed the first three steps in my 6 Ps methodology towards creating your corporate property strategy (the 'push' elements) and are now ready to move into the three 'pull' elements of the methodology. The first of these is the fourth P – Policies. The 2021 RICS guidance makes it clear that an asset management policy is a critical element of any asset management approach.[13] I agree.

Property strategy often fails because it lacks a clear policy framework. Without a clear policy framework, property staff will lack clarity on what is expected of them, colleagues outside the property function will not be clear on who does what and how decisions get taken, and decision-makers will have no firm reference point for decisions. Governance will be weak and decision-making will be poor or random.

There are three elements to the Policies step:

1. Divergence: Missing policies
2. Departure: Policy non-compliance
3. Devise: Developing new policy

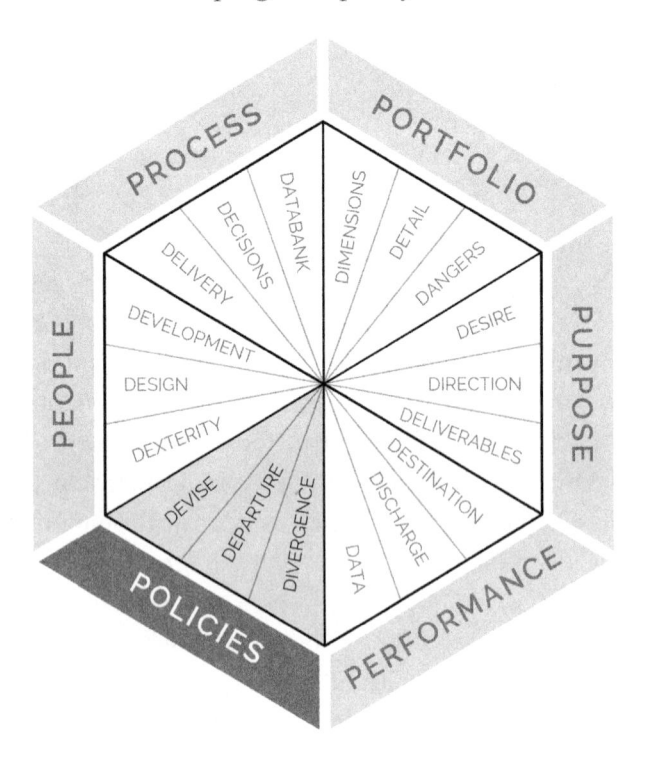

Divergence: Missing policies

Policies shape decisions, affect actions and set standards. In Chapter 2, I tasked you with compiling a list of the property policies in place within your organisation. Now is the time to revisit that list. Your initial step is to identify where your current policy framework diverges from the conclusions you reached on Purpose and Performance through the first three Ps. For example, if you identified a clear purpose for a part of the property portfolio, then you should have a written policy that says so. If you do not, then that is a policy divergence.

If you have identified a target area of performance and an associated performance gap, you will need a policy that will take you from current performance to target performance. Let's say, for example, you have set a target on net zero carbon. Without a clear, written statement that this is an organisational policy, staff and elected members may make decisions (some small and some potentially large) that will fight against your target. Do not attempt to write all the detailed policies now. Make a note of any areas of policy divergence and include them in your strategy. These become actions for strategy implementation. What you can write now is your strategic asset policy, which I discuss below.

The strategic asset policy element of any policy hierarchy consists of the overarching statements of management principles for the property portfolio as defined by the ISO 55000[14] standard. The second element of the policy hierarchy, organisational policies, focuses on broad authority, wide asset policies that need to be in place. These provide further detail to the strategic asset policy. The third element of the policy hierarchy contains the operational policies. These are going to be more 'local' in terms of the property function and need to be in place to ensure consistency in day-to-day operational estate management and to ensure the strategic policy and organisational policies are embedded in operational decisions and tasks. There may be a number of operational policies for each strategic policy, and there may be a number of organisational policies for each operational policy. The schematic in the diagram below shows this relationship.

It is important to get these policies right and to ensure you have a comprehensive policy suite at each of these levels. Policies shape decisions, affect actions and set standards.

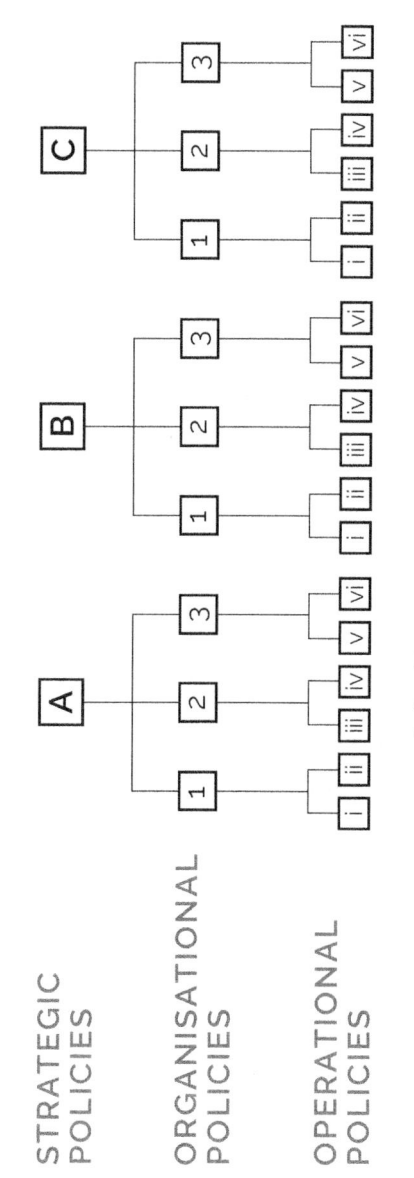

Policy hierarchy schematic

Strategic policy

The strategic asset policy is a set of principles an organisation will employ to meet objectives. Establishing a clear strategic asset policy which describes the management principles you aspire to is so important. Those who do not have a clear framework for how they expect their properties to be managed are continually reactive and have no moral compass to help shape decisions around their portfolio and influence decisions by property staff, service managers, directors and elected members.

The management principles I am talking about will not be the same for everyone, although I would expect to see similarities across the local government sector, given the similar nature of the organisations and the services provided to local communities. They may relate to environmental sustainability matters, social or community outcomes, property condition or financial performance matters – in fact, anything that reflects your portfolio purpose and which applies across the whole portfolio.

You could well review what others have done in this area, but these management principles – your strategic asset policy – needs to be unique to you. It should reflect your challenges. This is where the SWOT analysis you prepared in Chapter 3 will prove its worth. In this step, review your SWOT. You may want to pay particular attention to the strengths and weaknesses you identified. These are internal issues and more within your control to change.

Organisational policies

The organisational policy areas you need to have in your authority should be based on a) your property portfolio, b) the purpose of each portfolio segment and c) your performance expectations or aspirations. (In other words, all those things we have worked through in the preceding chapters.)

Some organisational policies will translate the strategic policy statement to show differentiation at a portfolio segment level. An example might include where you have a strategic policy statement that all property assets will be in 'good condition', but at an organisational policy level, how 'good' is defined may vary.

What you have in place currently may be inadequate, if you have policy statements at all. As a head of service once said to me, 'If you fail to prepare your policies, you prepare to fail your strategy.' I often hear people say there is no point in having a policy because elected members will only ignore it when decisions come to be taken. I do have some sympathy for that view, but it can create a self-fulfilling prophecy. In other words, you think you instinctively know what the policy should be and you apply it. Then situations come along where you argue for that 'policy' position, but decision-makers decide to take a different path. Your perception in that situation is that those decision-makers have gone against policy, but they haven't. What they have done is gone against what you thought the policy was – or should be. That is not the same thing at all. There was never an explicit policy. Your job is to create one. Having no policy framework is a recipe for chaos.

Property policies, in fact all policies, need to be owned not just by those that create them, but by those that apply them. Of course, it is the right of appointed decision-makers to depart from their own policy even when it is explicit, but I have found that if they understand the reason for a particular policy, elected members will take an active part in developing it, appreciate the consequences of departing from it, and more often than not, conform to it.

Other examples of organisational policies might include where and how property decisions get taken, who controls property budgets, if, where and when properties will be leased out or sold at less than market rates, policy standards around the condition of the property portfolio or net zero carbon. It might also include policies which cut across a number of departments, such as the granting of food and other concessions or public events on the authority's land.

Ultimately, you might be looking to create a compendium of these organisational property policies.

You should create a list of the areas where there is a need for an organisational property policy. Some of these policies may already be in place, others won't. Don't get distracted into starting to write the missing policies yet or you will never write your corporate property strategy. You can work through the policy drafting once your corporate property strategy has been adopted, but if you start now, you could find yourself writing the wrong policies with the wrong content.

CASE STUDY: POLICY CLARITY

I once facilitated a workshop for a local authority client on the topic of community asset transfer. The council had ambitions to support their local communities through greater community control of community assets and buildings. They didn't have a community asset transfer policy, despite the fact that good guidance on community asset transfer existed (including how to develop a policy). There were also plenty of examples of community asset transfer policies available in the public domain, many of which from neighbouring councils. When I asked why, given the council's ambitions, there was no policy on community asset transfer, I had an interesting range of responses. Some of their sentiments included:

- Members support community asset transfer, but it's not something the officer team are keen on.
- We have seen from elsewhere that asset transfer doesn't always work and when the group concerned

fails, organisations end up getting the asset back – often at great expense to the authority.
- Community asset transfer is great, as we can offload property assets that have become a bit of a burden for us.
- We wouldn't want to transfer high-value assets to the voluntary or community sector. These are public buildings paid for with the public purse. We might need to sell them at some point to raise capital.
- If we have a policy, then we will get forced into transferring assets that would not be in the best interests of the council.
- These asset transfers don't really work. They often rely on the assets being shared by multiple community groups, and when the groups end up falling out then the asset and the local community suffer.
- Community groups just want assets they can make money from, but don't want to pay for them.

As we worked through these concerns and explored examples of asset transfer that had happened in the absence of a policy anyway, the group were able to see that whatever their views or concerns were on community asset transfer, they would be met by having a clear policy. They now have a community asset transfer policy.

Operational policies

Alongside the broader organisation property policies, there will be a need to create a policy framework around day-to-day, operational property decisions. The purpose of these operational policies is not to influence strategic decisions by members or your asset management board, but by the property team. The larger the property team, the greater the risk that there will be an inconsistency in the way tasks are prioritised and decisions are made by that team.

Many of these operational policies will be connected to the strategic and organisational policies in your hierarchy. Examples of operational property policies might include such things as letting of grazing licences, tenant selection, standard lease covenants (such as FRI), rent-free periods, service charges, rent review frequencies, rent indexation or perhaps enforcement of encroachments. There will be many more possibilities than that, but hopefully this gives you some ideas.

The diagram below shows an example of the relationship between the three levels of the policy hierarchy and may help you in visualising policy relationships in other areas you will be considering.

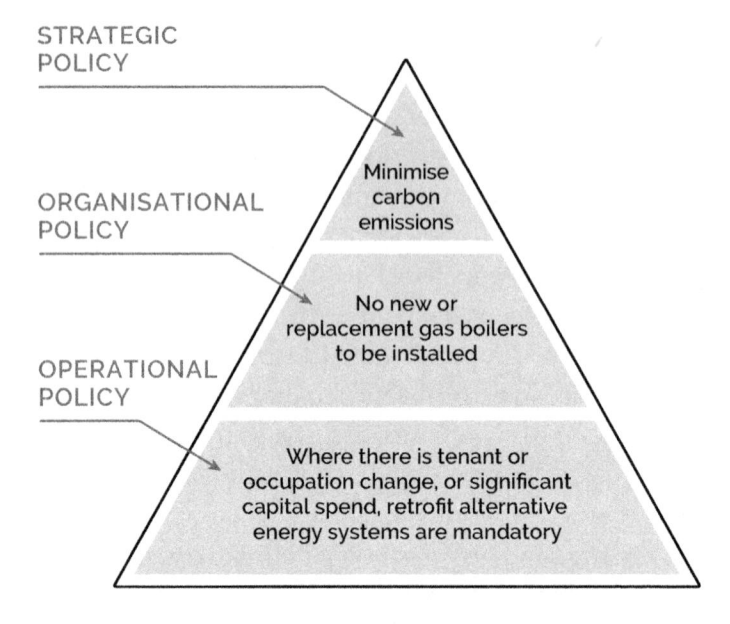

```
                    STRATEGIC
                    POLICY
                                          /\
                                         /  \
                                        /Minimise\
        ORGANISATIONAL                 / carbon  \
        POLICY                        / emissions \
                                     /─────────────\
                                    /   No new or   \
                                   / replacement gas \
                                  /  boilers to be    \
        OPERATIONAL              /     installed       \
        POLICY                  /───────────────────────\
                               /   Where there is tenant \
                              /    or occupation change,  \
                             /   or significant capital    \
                            /  spend, retrofit alternative  \
                           /   energy systems are mandatory  \
                          /_____\
```

The policy hierarchy relationships

Departure: Policy non-compliance

Writing a new property policy is easy, but if nobody knows about it or understands what it means and what it involves, it will be ignored by staff and decision-makers. The policy rules then get broken, and breaking policy rules can kill your strategy. On the occasions where I have seen significant and regular departure from property policies, it is more often than not because decision-makers were not involved in its development.

Let's look at an example. You take a policy report to a cabinet, board or committee agenda. It has been written by officers, there has been no meaningful previous dialogue and members of your board or cabinet have not been involved in shaping it. It is part of an extremely busy meeting agenda along with some rather weighty items. The report is well-written and all makes sense, so there is little discussion. Members are itching to get to the other agenda items which they might consider to be of greater importance. The policy is approved with little debate and you are happy because you get out of the meeting unscathed and without any grilling. You pat yourself on the back for a job well done.

You might believe the policy was approved because it is so well-written, but members approved it without having shaped it, without really having understood it and without fully understanding the consequences of it. Despite your introduction to the report, the policy might not have been fully explained to them. They quite possibly don't fully appreciate what the policy will really mean for future decisions they will be called on to make. You have relied on them having read your report and the policy and having fully understood it all, but they may in fact not be fully signed up to the ramifications of the policy they have just approved. When a future decision needs to be made, members have not properly bought into the policy. They do not really own it. It is easy for them to depart from it, because they do not fully understand the consequences of doing so. And depart from it they will. You will blame them for departing from it when that time comes, but the truth is that it is you that has failed and not them.

If you have an ineffective policy framework then your corporate property strategy will ultimately not deliver to its full potential. There is a need for honest reflection on how the organisation has treated property-related policies in the past. Have the policies been deployed properly? If not, what needs to happen to ensure compliance in the future? Think through your experiences within the organisation. Can you recall decisions being made that, to you, represent a departure from what you believed was established policy? Make a note of them. Then ask others to do the same – either on an individual basis or in a group setting. If you can do this successfully (and you will not identify everything first time around), then you will have identified some weaknesses in policy application that need addressing. Your corporate property strategy should be honest about these situations and identify actions that will address past policy departures.

The reasons for policy departure will vary. Perhaps people didn't know about the policy in question. It might be they thought the policy didn't have organisational backing and they wouldn't be supported in their decision or action. Perhaps the previous policy was badly drawn or unclear and needs to be rewritten or it is out of date and needs a thorough review (or can even be ditched altogether). It could be, in hindsight, the policy was completely unworkable and needs a thorough review. All property policies should be regularly reviewed and reaffirmed. Perhaps nobody knew the policy existed, and while it remains sound, you have work to do on communicating it. Maybe people are not applying the policy because they believe it didn't apply to their circumstances, in which case, again, improved communication may be needed.

Policy departure might be any number of other reasons. For every policy you and the team feel has been 'breached' in the past, set out the reasons you and they believe this happened. Write down what action you believe needs to be taken to prevent those breaches happening in the future. The important thing is to identify where this happened, identify why it happened and stop it happening again. If you can work through things in this way, you will have a list of policy reviews and communication activities that can be summarised in your corporate property strategy, and ultimately detailed in your delivery plan (or asset management plan).

Devise: Developing new policy

The third element of this P is to pull together all the policy divergence and departure issues into a list of required policy drafting. Do not allow yourself to start redrafting any policies at this stage. For the purposes of your corporate property strategy, you only need to know what policies need drafting. At this point, the list will have no shape or form. It might cover broad areas such as property condition, energy efficiency, business cases or community asset transfer. It might cover narrower areas such as standard lease terms, property investment criteria, garden land disposals, encroachments or granting food or filming concessions.

Your next task is to attach some priority to your list. Remember that this is a list of actions: a list of policies to be drafted and then adopted. There is no doubt that writing any policy and getting it adopted by an organisation is often no quick task. You might be daunted by your list and that is quite normal. Eventually you want to create a compendium of policies, but for now, you only want to prioritise the list and then you can spread the policy drafting over a sensible period of time.

It will be challenging for you to prioritise the policy drafting list, but the prioritisation is not entirely down to you. Engage with others, maybe your property team, management team or property board (if you have one) in helping with the prioritisation task. You may want to consider prioritising policy drafting that has the greatest positive impact on portfolio performance. Absent policies equal absent performance.

Procedures are not policies

Care needs to be taken to separate policy from procedures and processes, which we will examine in Chapter 8. I have seen plenty of documents purporting to be a policy which are either just procedural documents which explain how things happen in certain scenarios, or a mixture of policy and procedure. Where these kinds of documents exist, it is almost worse than having a written policy, as there can be confusion about what the real policy is.

For example, I was once asked to review a local authority's policy on property disposals at less than best consideration. First of all, it wasn't a policy, but a report to the management team. It had most likely not been shared beyond the management team and so had likely never been seen by elected members, the people that should have seen and approved it. The other thing that struck me was, of the twenty or so paragraphs of this 'policy', only around half actually contained any sort of policy statement. This was more of a statement to the management team of how the property team deal with enquiries for disposals at less than best consideration. It needed a great deal of work to turn it into a policy which could stand alone, bring clarity and be approved by members. This is far from the only example of poor policy drafting I have seen over my career. There is a skill to policy drafting.

There is nothing wrong with mixing policy and guidance, per se. Council Local Plans do this all the time. In fact, that was the model I adopted for a corporate land policy I developed at Bristol. If you are going to mix policy and guidance though, you must create a visual separation. There must be clarity of what the actual policy statements are. These, after all, are your rules. Any guidance woven among the policy statements should be explanations of how the policy will be applied.

Top tips

- Prepare the ground for policy prioritisation and development by capturing the main points of each of the intended new policies in bullet form against each policy title, explaining what the policy is about, why it is needed and what its aim is.

- Consider establishing policy development and scrutiny panels for elected members to assist with better policy making, understanding of policy implications and to oil the wheels of policy implementation and adherence.

- It may sound counterintuitive but making the circumstances where departure from policy may be considered clear in each policy can actually result in fewer policy departures.

Summary

By working through the actions in this chapter you have completed the fourth part of your corporate property strategy. You should now have a clear plan of what range of property policies are needed to deliver on your property purpose and property performance.

You have a prioritised list of policy drafting work. The prioritisation of the required property policies has potentially created a great deal of future work and actions. You need to spread these actions out over the life of your corporate property strategy, being clear on which you will be writing and adopting first and which will follow over the coming years. You should also think about whether this policy writing task is something you have the resources to complete in-house, or whether you need some external support.

You will most likely have identified such a long list of important property policies that you may be amazed at how the organisation has managed to operate effectively in the past. The likely truth is that it hasn't. That is why it is one of the Ps in the 6 Ps methodology.

SEVEN
People

You have used the three 'push' steps to fully understand your property portfolio before starting your journey home in the previous chapter with the first of the 'pull' steps (identifying the policy needs and gaps and setting a plan to tackle it).

The second 'pull' step is People. When it comes to developing a corporate property strategy, it is not enough to have good ideas, good advice and robust decision-making processes. Those are important, but without capacity and capability, even the best of corporate property strategies will never be implemented as intended.

There are three elements to the People step:

1. Dexterity: Designing around capabilities
2. Design: Getting the structure right
3. Development: Allow your people to grow

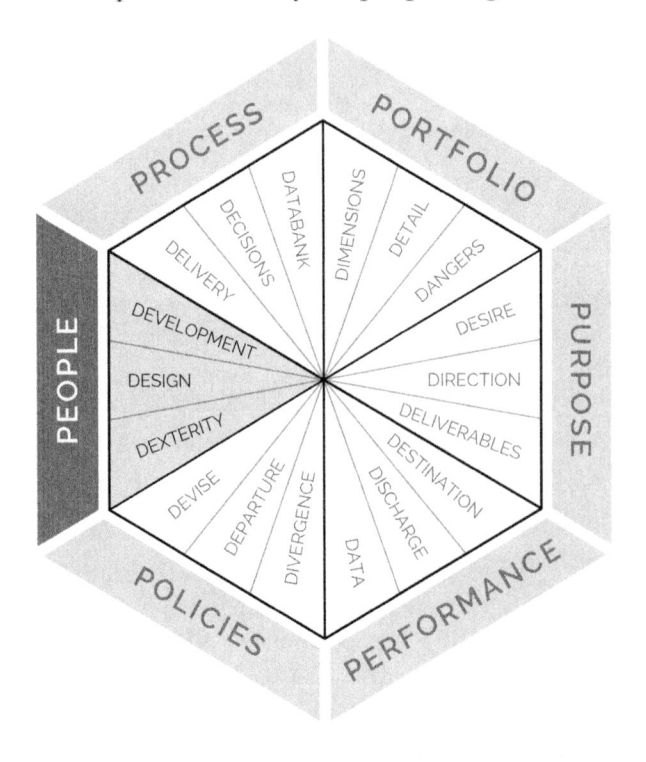

Dexterity: Designing around capabilities

Nothing happens in property strategy without people. It is not an automated process. You cannot use artificial intelligence to create it or implement it. It revolves around people's skills, knowledge, capabilities, and to a certain extent, motivation. You must know what skills, capabilities and knowledge you have in the team (or teams) so you know what you need to either bring in or develop to deliver your corporate property strategy.

Too many people leap to creating staffing structures and reporting lines without first thinking enough about what needs to be achieved. That is often because most thinking around structures tends to be dominated by operational requirements. Too little thinking is generally given to strategic outcomes, even though the ultimate goal of operational management is to deliver strategic goals. The result is often staff structures that don't look too different to the structures which preceded them. Often, I see similar numbers of estate surveyors, building surveyors, etc, that were there previously, but are just arranged in a slightly different way. Your staffing structures should not be shaped around what you already have and what you already do. They should be structured around your strategic needs and outcomes. Form should follow function.

There are a number of ways to assess people's skills, capabilities and knowledge. There is probably an entire book in explaining them, but you need to find your way of doing it. Of course, assessing skills and capabilities and developing people should never be a one-off activity. It should be a constant process. It has to be done sensitively and in a manner which prepares people for change.

One of the most difficult roles to fill can be strategic asset managers. Recruiting an estates surveyor, building surveyor or quantity surveyor, aside from the supply shortage issue, is fairly straightforward. These roles have been developed over many years, generally in a consistent way, and there is generally consensus across the industry about what each of them involves and what skills and capabilities are needed.

The asset manager role, on the other hand, is still in evolution. Many people (myself included) drift into a strategic role by some accident or twist of fate, or perhaps because of a behavioural style or way of thinking. An asset manager, in the strategic organisational sense, is a fairly late arrival in the evolution of the property profession. Strategic asset management in local government has only been around in any meaningful sense for around twenty years. When I got into such a role, I was already in my forties (my previous work and training having been in general practice surveying). Many of my counterparts were of similar age and not all came from general practice. We were the vanguard of this new discipline, arriving into asset manager roles largely because of the way we thought, rather than necessarily being great surveyors or engineers (although many were).

At that time, there was no qualification route to being a strategic asset manager. It was perhaps the ultimate in 'on-the-job' training. We learned from doing, because there was nobody before us to observe. As a head of service once said to me, 'Making mistakes was the best learning. We just didn't realise it back then.' We made loads of mistakes finding our way and working out what it meant to be an asset manager. I have been developing a competencies model for the past couple of years and I am pleased to share it with you for the first time in this book. There were iterations on the way and I am grateful for the two clients I was working with at the time for the feedback they gave me during its development – Durham County Council and Bristol City Council.

The competencies model set out in the diagram below can be read in the context of anyone in a strategic property role.

Feel free to make good use of it. The model might be useful to you in writing job roles, in the selection process for vacant strategic property roles and in people development. You may also find it useful in gaining clarity on the definition of an asset manager in your organisation. It might clarify the sort of relationship you expect your asset managers to have with internal clients and stakeholders, especially service managers. Please do not treat this model as fixed in stone. I urge you to change and adapt it so you can define the roles as you see them. Allow the roles to evolve further over time and amend the model as necessary.

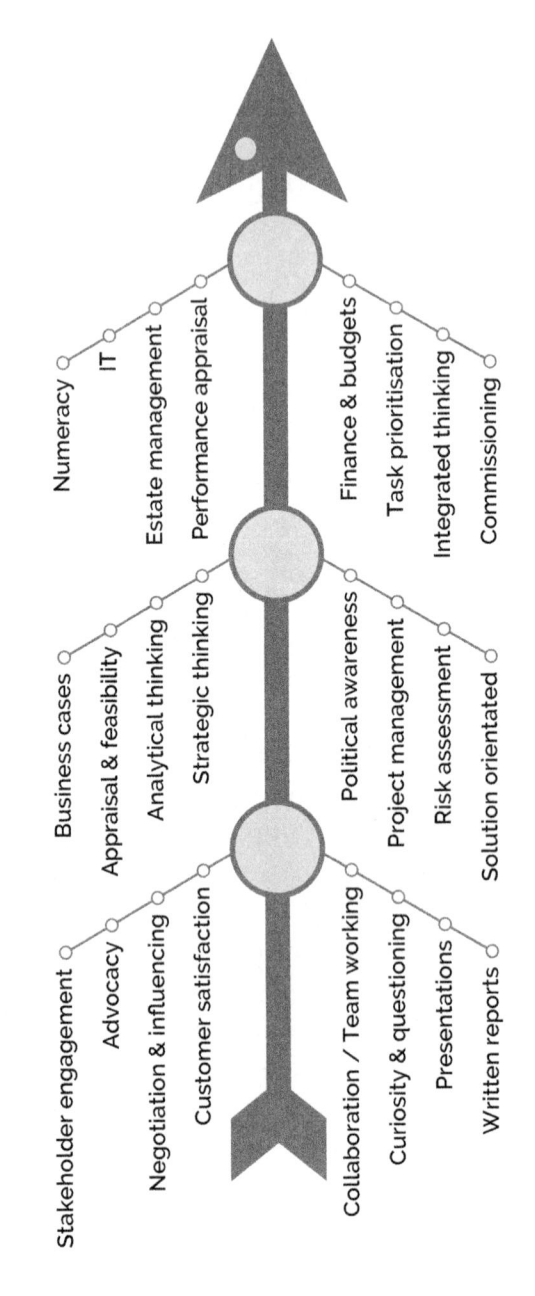

Competencies model

- Stakeholder engagement
- Advocacy
- Negotiation & influencing
- Customer satisfaction
- Collaboration / Team working
- Curiosity & questioning
- Presentations
- Written reports

- Business cases
- Appraisal & feasibility
- Analytical thinking
- Strategic thinking
- Political awareness
- Project management
- Risk assessment
- Solution orientated

- Numeracy
- IT
- Estate management
- Performance appraisal
- Finance & budgets
- Task prioritisation
- Integrated thinking
- Commissioning

What you will see in this competencies model is that the role is one of support and guidance, as much as a forward-thinking one. It is a core internal role for the organisation, but has the characteristics of a consultancy role.

CASE STUDY: JOB TITLES

One local authority I have been working with has fully embraced this thinking about property roles and job titles. They are not using the term 'surveyor' or 'valuer'. These titles can often imply the roles are transactional in nature, rather than fulfilling a strategic purpose. Nor are they using the job title of 'asset manager'. This has been adopted by so many different parts of the property profession that it has started to lack definition. Instead, their senior property roles are described as 'consultant surveyors'. This shakes off the shackles of historic job titles, makes a statement about a fresh start for these property roles, better frames what the roles involve, and hopefully, will start the process of changing mindsets of those in these roles.

Design: Getting the structure right

Fragmentation brings dysfunctionality. Having considered the dexterity, or capabilities, needed, you now need to create a staffing structure. There is a need to decide how the property functions of the organisation will be arranged to deliver a property service, and thus, the corporate property strategy. There is also a need to determine how the team structures will best support property users and occupiers, as well as the wider organisation.

I am only talking about a corporate landlord to a certain extent. The term 'corporate landlord' – one which I personally despise – is more about your governance model. The governance aspects of a corporate landlord are something I will talk about in Chapter 8. For now, I am interested in how the property functions are arranged, how fit for purpose they are and how they operate as a cohesive unit. It is not necessary to assume the current structures must automatically be wrong. They may not be, but they should be challenged and reviewed. Tinkering with the staffing structures may be all that is needed. In other situations, where the new organisational strategy sets a completely new property direction, wholesale change may be appropriate. Every organisation and situation will be different.

I have seen all manner of different staffing structures – quite possibly as many structures as I have had clients. Where many clients go wrong is devising the property team structure in a vacuum. Changes to staffing structures must have a good business case. Getting staffing structures right needs an understanding of the portfolio, its purpose, its expected performance and the policy framework. You also need to stand back and consider the capabilities needed, particularly the level of strategic thinking it takes at all levels, to deliver a corporate property strategy. If you restructure your property teams in a vacuum, you will not be surprised to learn it will not serve you as well as if you had based the team structure on what the organisation needs. What you need is a team structured around the strategic objectives, the performance objectives and the policy objectives.

It should be acknowledged that any property structure must fit in with the organisational structure. That may be outside of your control, but through this process you may be able to exert some influence on what the property elements of that organisational structure should look like.

Is there an ideal or perfect structure? Yes, there is, but what is perfect for one organisation will be a misfit for the next. It will depend on what the outcomes and outputs were from the first four Ps in this book. In my experience, where any one of the property functions reports to a different manager or director, you see dysfunctionality. The level and seriousness of dysfunctionality will vary depending on the extent of the separation of the various property teams and the qualities of the managers or directors involved, but it is inevitable. The managers or directors involved may not see dysfunctionality. Their focus is on running the service or services they manage. Others will see it. It might be other managers and directors, or property staff further down the hierarchy. It may be people in service departments, but dysfunctionality will be there and it will manifest itself somehow. Because levels of dysfunctionality vary so much, you will have to carefully work through and develop your business case.

Before you launch into any property reorganisation, you should note that research suggests over 80% of reorganisations fail to deliver their full objectives.[15] In my view, the ideal structure involves bringing all your property functions under a single manager or director. Typical property functions might include estates surveyors, buildings surveyors, architects, designers, quantity surveyors, building engineers, facilities managers and construction project managers. These functions may be delivered in-house, outsourced or delivered through joint ventures or arms' length trading entities. I appreciate views on this will vary. For me, a single, cohesive property function means everything will operate more smoothly, teams will collaborate in a way they didn't when they were separate, resources can be deployed across teams and there is a shared goal in delivering a seamless property service to the organisation and to property users and occupiers. There are also benefits to work processes and systems.

I am not going to get into a deep discussion around insourcing or outsourcing here, but it might well be a consideration for you. Getting the right balance between what functions are undertaken in-house and which are outsourced is important. Often, a mixture is the most efficient solution, as it can cope better with peaks and troughs in workload. Part of your task is to also consider whether the team have the tools and established processes to get their jobs done efficiently, as that can also influence the number of people the team needs.

Thinking of the staff structure as fixed in time will hold you back. Be prepared to be fluid. There is a temporal aspect to property team staff structures which is not always compatible with the way some public sector organisations operate. The number of people needed is subject to so many variables. These include the nature of the property portfolio, the distribution of the portfolio in relation to the land area of the authority, the policy framework, financial and other performance targets being demanded of the team, the quality of the tenants and their ability to pay rent and meet other lease obligations without prompting, the number of public and member enquiries the team receive, and even down to the specific lease terms. That is quite a lot to take into account.

Structure benchmarking

It is worth mentioning the role benchmarking sometimes plays in staff reorganisations. Many local authorities are tempted into comparing their staffing structures and property budgets with other local authorities. I am not saying you should not do that, but you should take care how you do it and the lessons you take from it. As the authors of *Reorg: How to Get it Right* say, this kind of anonymous benchmarking 'encourages a "rush to the bottom"'.[16] Such benchmarking is extremely difficult to reliably calibrate between organisations. There are ways of comparing a service in one authority with other services in other authorities, but this can be clumsy. The main reason is that property portfolios vary so much from organisation to organisation, as do the strategic property objectives and the starting point of each organisation. Remember that there are multiple variables that have shaped the size of the team in your organisation, as they have the size of teams in comparison organisations. Simple comparison cannot tell you what you should do. That you have to decide for yourself, but some form of comparison can be informative at a high level.

Development: Allow your people to grow

Staff development and motivation should always be an ongoing process of understanding and meeting business and personal needs. It is an integral part of the people structure. In recent years, funding for staff training and development across the public sector has dwindled. It is routinely a budget that comes under attack when savings need to be made. In my view, this is one of the biggest false economies that any organisation can engage in.

All the great work you have achieved so far in following the methodology in this book will be lost if you do not equip and develop your people to do the job for you. If you have followed my steps, you should now have a full picture of what the organisation wants from its property portfolio. You may, by now, have also started to form a view on what your property team structure should look like, and what skills you need to get the job done and the strategy delivered.

People need to love work to do great work. This means tapping into people's motivation for work. The opportunities for bonus structures in local government are next to zero, so immediate or short-term motivation through money is not likely to be available to you. In any case, many people entering local government may not necessarily be motivated by financial reward.

Team structure

The team structure can provide great motivation. The right team structure, showing a career progression path – even in small steps – can be highly motivating. It can encourage people to come out of their shells and take on tasks outside of the defined scope of their current roles. This relies on a positive workplace culture where expression is not only valued, but encouraged.

There has been a tendency over the years to adopt so-called 'flat' structures. These are often seen as being efficient and also saving money, as you have fewer 'managers'. I am not certain this trend has served the sector well in all situations. It has often resulted in spans of control which are too broad. If this is a policy of your organisation, you may be constrained in the hierarchal nature of the staffing structure you are allowed to create. The trick in this situation is to use the 'flatter' structure in a creative way and create career progression roles (sometimes called 'career grades') which allow room for people development. These are something people can visualise. They can picture themselves five years from now, having more responsibility, maybe including an element of team-leader supervision or mentoring and, yes, perhaps more money.

Devising the staffing structure is not just a 'how many of what' task. You need to consider the motivational aspects of the structure and how these will help you develop your property team. One motivating factor is simply interesting work. For those in the public sector especially, finding ways to show people the bigger picture and how their contribution is making things happen can be huge. When people feel they are part of something bigger than themselves, motivation levels increase.

Collaboration develops people, too. Avoiding task-thinking and encouraging project-thinking can make a big difference to staff motivation and development. People will develop new skills in a project context and they will also develop new relationships with others in all parts of the organisation.

Strategic thinking

Consistency of definition and understanding traditional property roles can be helpful, but it can also be a hindrance. What is needed in any role depends on context. In a public sector organisation trying to deliver against a strategy, property surveyors need skills and capabilities beyond their traditional training. They need political awareness and they need a public sector ethos, but these two things are not enough.

Surveyors also need strategic awareness. It is often strategic awareness that is missing from the DNA of the average surveyor. Strategic awareness demands that people be inquisitive and have the ability to see the bigger picture. There must be an appreciation that the task is about providing property resources to support service delivery and not about managing property assets. In the development of your corporate property strategy, I urge you to not only think about how many strategic roles you need, but how you will get everyone thinking strategically. Much of that is down to mindset, habits and behaviours – and that's another book on its own.

Top tips

- Do not think of the staffing structure as fixed in time, but as a blueprint telling you what property team resources you need to get the job done and get the strategy delivered.

- If the 'defragmentation' of the property functions into a single team is not possible in your organisation, you could consider interim arrangements as a first step to build linkages across disparate teams through working groups.

- Try to be creative with job titles, perhaps using things like 'consultancy surveyor' rather than tired, traditional job titles.

Summary

In this chapter, we have looked at the need to understand the people element of creating your corporate property strategy, including the skills and competencies you need and the staffing structure you need. Please do not underestimate the role your people (at all levels) will play in seeing your strategy delivered.

In the next chapter – the final P of my 6 Ps – we will look at the processes you will have to develop to achieve your ambitions for your property portfolio. You will need a balance of day-to-day operational processes and strategic governance processes.

EIGHT
Process

In this chapter of my 6 Ps methodology, I am going to take you through the final piece to get you to your corporate property strategy – Process. There is an awful lot which can be said about processes. Developing them can be difficult. Keeping them simple is, too. Staff don't follow them. Senior people don't want to be constrained by them. Politicians override or ignore them. Stage-left events render them redundant. Whatever your processes, they need to be easily changed, because times change.

If you have identified actions against the other five Ps in this book, then this will necessitate changes to processes, procedures, decision-making and data. You will not necessarily find solutions immediately.

THE PROPERTY STRATEGY HANDBOOK

You should make a note of what you already have in place and what needs to be in place. It is important you build on the work you have done and identified through the other chapters.

There are three elements to the Process step:

1. Delivery: Strengthening operating procedures
2. Decisions: Strengthening governance
3. Databank: Tools of the trade

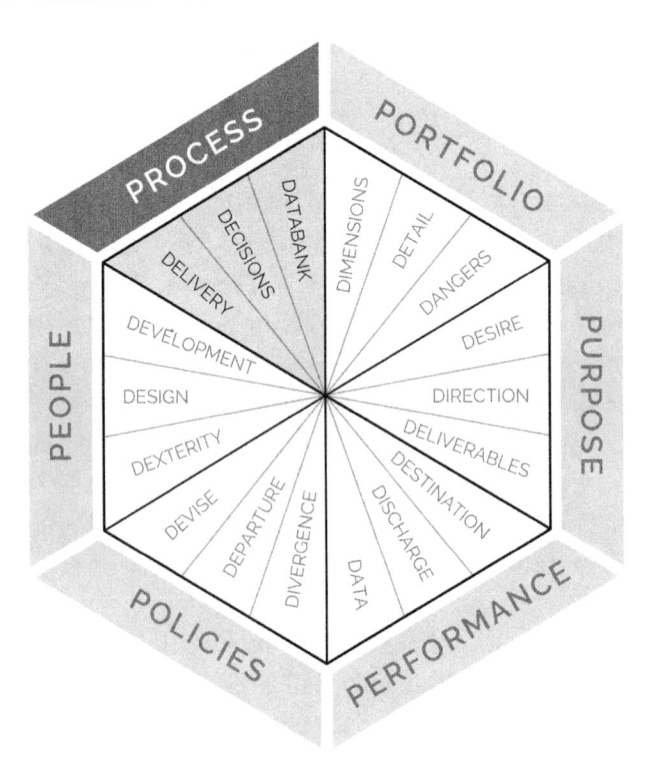

Delivery: Strengthening operating procedures

The first step in this P is around how the property team operate. In the previous chapter, we looked at skills and competencies, used this to get you thinking about a new property team structure and also how you develop and motivate your people. The gains from that process will not materialise if you do not now review operating processes and procedures.

You may be looking to bring together disparate property teams that were previously under multiple managers or directors. Each of those operating units would have had their own internal procedures. The way things were done in each unit or team will carry the characteristics of that unit or team, operating in semi-isolation from other property units and teams. Those procedures will also have the hand of the previous manager or director on them. You need cohesive procedures for all parts of the property team which are tasked with delivering your corporate property strategy. That is not to criticise previous procedures. There may well have been reason for them in the previous context, but this is a new world you are helping to create and you need new procedures to go along with that.

You will hopefully have identified a fresh and clear direction for the property portfolio, a new approach to property performance management and a set of new property policies and standards that need applying. This demands you develop new standard operating procedures. Standard operating procedures might include simple things like what happens when someone applies to take a lease on a property or what happens at the end of a lease. In both those examples, a number of different property professionals might be involved, including estate surveyors, a building surveyor, a quantity surveyor or engineer, people in the property database team, as well as colleagues in both finance and legal. Each case will involve different people. Without clearly documented procedures, there is scope for inconsistency. Inconsistency creates inefficiency. Standard operating procedures should be in place for every operational process.

There are a number of scenarios you may face when you begin this task. The most challenging is where operating procedures are patchy and not well-formed, or worst of all, not documented at all. Where written procedures are blurry or non-existent, this means there is every chance people are operating multiple operating procedures for the same task. You could ask everyone involved in each specific task or activity to independently document the way they undertake their part of that particular task. They might need some coaching before they start, as documenting procedures is not a skill everyone has. By comparing procedures, you will immediately identify similarities and divergence on the same activity.

You could then facilitate a discussion to work through each step and devise an agreed procedure together. This will identify where people have incorrectly drawn the procedure they follow (which is likely to happen, by the way). It will also highlight the misalignment and generate discussion about what the best, or most efficient, procedure is. Do not underestimate the value of allowing people undertaking tasks to find new ways of doing things. They will have it in them. Perhaps they have just never been asked or maybe they previously operated within an environment that did not actively encourage suggestions.

Service modernisation and innovation are key to developing new ways of working. The pandemic has clearly shown us the need to find new ways of working or to try out new ways of doing things for the benefit of customers.

You may find your procedures are already well-documented in some areas. There are staff handbooks or worksheets. There may even be flowcharts. That is a great starting point if that is the case. That is not to say these things do not need changing, because they most likely will, but you will find it much easier to review them because you know what they are and everyone should be following them. I say 'should' because it might be that not everyone is following them. Reviewing existing documented procedures begins a communication process to remind (or tell) people they exist – once, of course, you have made any necessary adjustments. Tap into existing knowledge and the day-to-day obstacles people face and get them involved in the review of the procedures. You will be glad that you did.

Bear in mind that you are on the journey of creating your corporate property strategy. At this stage, it is simply enough to identify which procedures are in place and may need reviewing, and which processes are not yet documented and need creating. Specific actions will become part of your delivery plan (or asset management plan) and will be delivered over time, depending on the priorities you attach to them. And prioritise them you should. The task of writing new procedures is resource hungry. If you allow it, it will become a massive distraction and your corporate property strategy will never get written, let alone implemented.

CASE STUDY: PROCESS MAPPING

I was working with a county unitary recently to help them to refine and improve the procedures and process around the sale of land to local residents to extend their gardens. Sales were taking too long and applicants were complaining to their ward councillors and MPs, who were then complaining to the head of service and the chief executive.

The task was how to establish the most efficient process – one that made the process faster so complaints were reduced and everyone was more contented. Through process mapping, the steps were broken down to identify duplication of effort, points where people involved did not need to be, where tasks could be run in parallel rather than sequentially and where some tasks could start earlier in the process to save time later.

The outcome was a leaner, quicker process, shaving weeks from the previous timeline for the activity. I produced a small leaflet setting out the stages of the process to be sent to those applicants enquiring right at the start. This manages expectations by setting out steps and likely timescales and provides a constant reference point on progress. By providing up-front cost and timescale indications, the number of applicants proceeding beyond the initial approach stage has dropped dramatically.

Decisions: Strengthening governance

Much good work on strategic property asset management can be lost because of the way decisions in the organisation are made. Clear governance involving good strategy, policies and processes provides you with a golden thread which is critical for successful strategy implementation. Strong governance means strong strategy.

There is a saying, 'The way you do one thing is the way you do everything.' I have found this to be true in local government. Organisations that are guilty of poor decision-making in property asset management are often guilty of poor decision-making elsewhere.

A business mentor of mine has a maxim: 'Environment dictates performance'. This is so true with local authority decision-making. The organisational environment often determines how property decisions are made. We are the product of, and influenced by, the environment around us. If we see decisions being made elsewhere in the organisation which do not go through a proper business case process, we are less likely to do so with property decisions.

This is your opportunity to not only strengthen the decisions around the property portfolio, but through doing so, to also influence others. They will be influenced by the decision-making discipline you introduce. Believe me. I have seen it happen. The question you need to ask yourself is, 'What is a robust decision-making process, and how do I factor that into my corporate property strategy?'

You need a formal property decision-making forum. I recommend that this be made up of officers. You will need it to drive and oversee progress in both creating and delivering your corporate property strategy. You need it up and running as soon as possible, if you do not already have one. If you already have such a forum, rename it. This is a new start and you need everyone to realise it. You will be surprised at what a difference that can make. My preference would be something like 'Property Board', but the choice is yours. It matters more what it does and how it does it.

You may have just muttered to yourself, 'Such officer boards cannot make decisions.' You would technically be right. Local government constitutions do not generally allow officer working groups to make decisions – only properly constituted committees with elected members can do that – but a property board is, and should be, a key element of your decision pathway process in terms of property decisions and use of delegated powers.

How do you square the circle? You need the board to 'effectively' make decisions. How you achieve that will turn on a number of things. In fact, there are five things, which I call the 'Property Board Disciplines'. These must all be in place for there to be an effective and efficient property board. They are:

Attendance discipline: Organisations often make the mistake in believing property asset management involves making collective decisions. It does not. To be great at property asset management, and to be truly strategic, decisions need to be made by those with the ability to make strategic decisions. This false belief often results in organisations having as many people as possible involved in property decision-making. After all, such decisions can impact lots of people – especially if this is part of remodelling the way a service is delivered, reshaping the office accommodation portfolio, deciding which service should occupy a particular building or deciding how a particular vacant site should be used. As a consequence, many organisations form large property boards, attended by representatives of the main service areas. In larger organisations, this often means bloated groups being created. You work in a democracy, and you democratise property decision-making. Perfectly understandable, but in my experience, not such a great idea.

Parkinson's Law on the coefficient of inefficiency advocates that committees (or boards or cabinets) should be limited to only five people.[17] Moves to expand beyond five people should be resisted. Others can be asked to attend for specific items from time to time, but they should be occasional attendees for a specific purpose or agenda item. This makes the meetings far more effective. I am not saying you necessarily have to be strict with a limit of five property board members, but you should impose a limit. You need the most senior people on your property board. That should, as a minimum, include finance and legal representatives. If you are going to extend invitations to service managers, stick to directors or assistant directors, and then only those of the larger services. They wield the power, influence and authority you need to get the right decisions made. They are more likely to think strategically, and will be less wedded to individual service areas because of their broad spans of responsibility and position within the structure. Allow others at service manager level to be consulted of course, but do not allow them to be a regular part of the strategic decision-making process. If you do, you will find yourself too often walking through treacle as you go around in circles experiencing decision inertia. Your task is to make the case for a truly strategic property board with the right people involved.

Decision discipline: If your corporate property strategy is to sustain itself, you need a robust decision pathway. This is essential if the organisation is to make sound judgements and recommendations leading to sound decisions. It is important to have the property board recognised as a critical officer group. There needs to be an unequivocal decision pathway from the inception of ideas or the identification of challenges through business case development to a final decision. That decision pathway must involve the property board on every occasion. There must be no occasions where property-related matters loop around the property board and go straight to cabinet. Short-cuts, if allowed to happen, will simply encourage more people to take more short-cuts. It will create precedents you will regret later down the road. If you are in a local authority with a committee system rather than a cabinet system, or operate in a police or fire authority, you need to find a similar way to fit your property board into your governance structure. There should ideally be a supporting structure in place within committee services to pick up inadvertent attempts to take reports to cabinet or other committees without the matter being seen by the property board. Your task is to protect the organisation from itself. It needs firm discipline. It needs constant enforcement and reinforcement, or organisational standards will slip.

Agenda discipline: The agenda and minutes of a property board can be a real eye-opener. Pull up the latest minutes from your most recent meeting and you may see what I mean. Too often, the agenda is dominated by progress updates on specific schemes or projects. If the board was set up with terms of reference that set out its strategic purpose, it has likely lost its way. It has lost sight of that strategic purpose and gravitated back to talking about things that the people on the board like to talk about because they find it interesting. The board is not there to give people interest in their work. It is there to make strategic decisions. It is good practice to adopt a forward plan for the property board which should be reviewed at every meeting, and if possible, tied in with your cabinet timetable (if you operate a cabinet system). You do need clear strategic terms of reference, but the board needs to be managed well so it sticks to its remit. A good secretariat support to the property board will ensure decisions are documented.

CASE STUDY: TRIAGE

One of my clients adopted an innovative element to the discipline of controlling the agenda of their strategic property decisions. They called it the 'triage'. Similar to the triage process you might see in a medical environment, it assigns degrees of urgency to the board agenda. Individual property officers are allocated to individual operational units within the service, much like you might see with finance business partners in the local government context.

The role of those individuals is to work closely with their operational colleagues and support them in presenting to the board property assets issues that need a board decision as part of the governance process. This organisation has even set up a dedicated 'triage' email address where proposals and business cases are submitted. That support network provides three main benefits:

- It helps operational managers to appreciate what information the board will need in reaching a decision, including the nature and depth of any business case which will be required.
- It helps those operational managers to understand the organisational context within which decisions around property get taken and helps to embed a corporate landlord model.
- It helps the board reach decisions efficiently, as all the information they need is provided and they do not waste time discussing items which have not yet been sufficiently well-developed. As such, it is an effective 'screening' process for ideas or initiatives unlikely to have a firm business case.

Any agenda screening process is not simply a case of reading through a draft report to validate that it is ready for the board to see. If you have a good corporate landlord model in place (or property partnership model, as I prefer to call it), the property team will include property strategy business partners who are assigned to service managers to help them develop property-related ideas and respond to property-related challenges. They have a key role in the screening process and should be well-drilled in both the role of the property board and the minimum standards for any report going to the board. This will help ensure the board sees only well-formed ideas, making the decision role so much easier.

Business case discipline: One reason local authorities make poor property decisions is that the decision is made before the business case is written. People often work backwards from the answer they want and then use this to justify the case for it. Everyone knows this is bad practice and everyone knows it happens. Forming or renaming your property board (with fresh terms of reference) is a fantastic opportunity to bring the business case discipline back to the fore. The property board should not be reaching any decision without a written business case. This does not have to be a heavy, full business case for every decision. Some decisions can be made with less detailed information, but even in these cases, there should be a structure and a discipline about the way the decision is made. By far the best way to do that is to have business case templates.

The UK Government's recommended business case approach is the 'Five Case Model'.[18] There is a danger with such models that organisations seeking to implement them will create an unnecessary business case industry. You do not want to fall into that trap. While things like the Five Case Model provide a discipline and structure to arrive at the best possible decision, it is not a substitute for judgement and experience – these will always be required at various points in any decision-making process. Nevertheless, the Five Case Model is a sound discipline, with a good structure which picks up the five main areas that a business case should include, namely: the Strategic Case, the Economic Case, the Commercial Case, the Financial Case and the Management Case. I would recommend you develop personalised templates for your property board, perhaps based on the Five Case Model, but acknowledging there will be a need for differing degrees of depth and complexity.

Reporting discipline: The business case approach above is a key element of the reporting process, but reporting discipline is more than about presenting business cases. There needs to be a reporting discipline that supports both the business case discipline and the agenda discipline. The three areas are closely linked. The reporting discipline is about:

- The form the reports take.

- The subject matter of the reports fitting the terms of reference.

- The timeliness of reporting (to avoid rushed decision-making).

- The repetition of reporting where required, such as performance reports or progress on strategy implementation.

- The follow-up reporting, where the board has asked for further information or reports on matters it has previously seen.

- The timely publication of agendas and reports.

- Recording and timely publication of meeting minutes and action points.

- Chasing up those responsible for action points and follow-up reports.

A good reporting discipline will help the board avoid verbal reports, which weaken both the transparency of the governance process and the decision audit trail. Succinct reports are best, maybe with a three-slide PowerPoint introduction to summarise what the board is being asked to decide, it being assumed everyone has already read the full report.

Databank: Tools of the trade

A database is a single computer system holding information. The 'holy grail' of having an all-embracing property database fulfilling all the needs of property practitioners and the organisation is unlikely to be achieved. It is best to realise that early on. Instead of aspiring to a single database, you are better aspiring to a 'databank'. The Oxford Languages definition of a databank is, 'A large repository of computer data on a particular topic, sometimes formed from more than one database, and accessible by many users'. In other words, a databank is the totality of information, not necessarily a single system. I use the term 'databank' as an approach to data management which provides reliable and timely information on the property portfolio to those that need it.

Property data should not be regarded as the possession of the property team. It is information belonging to the whole organisation which is critical to decision-making. It is organisational information and should be structured and available to everyone needing it. Your task is to create a databank that fits the needs of your organisation. I say that, as the chances are that you do not have this at the moment. You quite possibly have multiple computer systems that do not talk to one another. Some of the property data you need is held in systems managed by the property team, but not all of it. Some data is held in finance or other systems. Your data will be incomplete, possibly because the data does not exist or has never been collected. Maybe the data exists and you always intended to populate your property database with it, but never quite got around to it. There is a Chinese proverb that says something along the lines of, 'The best time to plant a tree was twenty years ago. The second-best time is now.' The same goes for your databank.

Your task is to undertake an audit of where property-related data currently sits, identify who manages data and how up to date it is, identify duplicated data, identify how data gets into systems and test sample data for quality and reliability. One thing to be aware of if you secure a dedicated resource to review and audit your data is that the process may take several years to complete. I would love to tell you it won't, but it will. The earlier you make a start, the better. You should reflect this in your staffing structure. You might also consider whether you need data analysis capability to support both the identification of data requirements and performance management and reporting.

Pull this information into a report setting out the strengths and weaknesses of the current arrangements and which sets out a blueprint for your new databank arrangements. Key elements for any databank include:

- Data manager
- Data collection processes
- Data access
- Data cleansing and reconciliation
- Data reporting
- Data quality
- Data updating
- Data connectivity

If you can establish a sound databank, the day-to-day lives of operational property professionals, property strategists, service managers, elected members, directors and the property board will be transformed. All organisations rely on great data. In this digital age, data, and how we manage, use, analyse and manipulate it, will grow in importance. You need a databank which gives you the information infrastructure essential in property strategy, property management and strategic decision-making.

Top tips

- When devising or reviewing processes, keep the portfolio purpose, your performance framework and your policy framework in mind and what will best deliver your corporate property strategy.

- Plan ahead on where you will keep and maintain adopted processes and how people will access them. Obstacles to access is often an excuse for non-compliance.

- When creating or re-branding your property board, put a communication plan in place to ensure board members and others understand their respective roles and responsibilities.

Summary

I have stressed the importance of processes. Whether those processes relate to property operational procedures, governance arrangements or your databank, they are all equally important. If you can get this element right, the sum of the whole is most certainly greater than the sum of the parts. These are big tasks I have set you.

There is no magic bullet. There is no overnight success. There may have been a lightbulb moment in reading this chapter where you realised some of the weaknesses in your organisation's approach. You may have identified some areas where your organisation is going wrong. A key step in making change is realising that change is needed. You now need to make a plan to bring about that change.

PART THREE
GETTING IT DONE

Reading this book is one thing. Taking action is another. That is what Part Three of this book is about. It is as important as everything that has gone before. Please do not skip the chapter thinking you have absorbed what the 6 Ps are all about and you are ready to begin the strategy writing process. You are not.

NINE
Making A Start

In Chapter 2, I talked about having a strategic mindset and preparing yourself and others for the task ahead. Now that you know what faces you in preparing your property strategy, you need to keep the energy levels high to maintain momentum of action, know how to prioritise your tasks and keep checking where you are on your journey.

First night nerves

Writing a corporate property strategy – especially a great one – is not for the faint-hearted. I won't lie to you, it is a challenge. There's a lot to ask of yourself. Do I have the capability to write it? Will I be able to manage the project and keep it moving? How will

I cope with facilitating workshops and group discussions? Will I encounter resistance with some people not playing ball? Will the information I need be available? And most of all, where on earth will I find the time to do all this?

If you're nervous, the truth is that it's a good thing. Believe me, there is not a performer out there, no matter how accomplished, who does not have a rush of adrenaline before going on stage. As a musician, I have first-hand experience of that. 'Aah,' you say, 'a musician is different. They have practised and rehearsed for the performance, so they know what they are doing.'

I get it. Perhaps you are going into this for the first time. You haven't practised and rehearsed a corporate property strategy. I remember when I first became a property trainer and consultant. My first presentation was in London in February 2003. I was as nervous as hell. I had never given any kind of formal presentation before. I hadn't been recruited for my presentation skills; I had been recruited because of my knowledge of strategic property asset management. I woke up feeling sick. I felt sick on the two-hour train journey from Bristol to London. I felt sick on the Tube from Paddington to St James's Park. I felt sick the whole morning through to when the time came to give my presentation.

I remember the presentation well. It was called 'Sense and Suitability'. I had reviewed a number of different

MAKING A START

asset suitability approaches and my presentation was to explain these different approaches and talk about the pros and cons of each. Also speaking that day was CIPFA Associate, Alan Tyler. He had been presenting for a good number of years and seemed to be a polished presenter. He took me aside just before the first presentation and gave me some great advice. 'Always remember,' he said, 'the audience will never know what you didn't say.' It was simple advice, but just what I needed. I was so worried I would miss something out and it would ruin the presentation, but Alan was right. The audience only sees and hears what you do and say. They don't know if you miss something out, so they won't judge you for it.

Why am I telling you this story? With the corporate property strategy task ahead of you, you will be judged by what you do, not by what you don't do. It is unlikely you will have anyone else in your organisation who has written a corporate property strategy before. (If you do, then get them to work with you on it.) Nobody else will know what is involved. You will be driving this project. People will, of course, look to you to move it forward and engage the right people at the right time. They will look to you because, in their eyes, you are the expert.

Equipped with this book, you have the framework, approach and tools to get this corporate property strategy written. You may not get everything right all of the time. Don't worry, nobody does. Plates will stop spinning and balls will be dropped. That's quite normal. There will be times when you feel it is all going wrong. It isn't. (There will also be times when you think it is all going right, but it isn't.) You just need to keep your balance and realise that writing a corporate property strategy is not about winning or losing. It is about the journey.

Action, not hope

One thing for certain about a corporate property strategy is that it will not happen because you wish it to happen. A corporate property strategy is built on action, not hope. You have to put the work into this project and so do other people. That is why in the earlier part of this book I spent so much time talking about preparation. If you did your preparation well and you have grasped the interlocking importance of the 6 Ps, you will have an excellent chance of creating a great corporate property strategy. You have the mindset and framework to work from. I have hopefully taken away some of your misgivings with this book and given you the confidence that you can do this if you follow a clear methodology, but the strategy will not write itself.

During the process of implementing this book, you will have captured the achievements and goals (what you have in place) and the gaps and unknowns (what you don't yet have in place) from each of the six Ps.

This will have brought you to a position of knowing where you are, and where you want to be. Believe me, this is a place not everyone gets to. Some people are so busy imagining the end of the journey that they forget to orientate themselves properly, so they don't know where they are. If you know the destination, but you don't know the starting point, you will be in for an unfulfilling journey. On the other hand, some people spend a great deal of time establishing where they are and then set off on their journey with no real direction. If they get to where they might have wanted to be had they properly thought about it, it will be through chance rather than planning. My aim in this book has been to provide you with a framework which helps you to strike the balance between these two things: to understand where you are and also to set yourself a clear destination.

Priorities

Everyone reading this book will be in a slightly different place. No two organisations are identical. Putting aside local politics, every organisation's challenges are different. The resources available to them are different. The property portfolio they have is different. The demographics of local communities is different. The local economies are different. The topography of the landscape is different. The size of the population and the area the organisation serves is different.

When it comes to strategic property asset management, organisations will also be in a different place. Some will be further ahead than others. Having worked though the 6 Ps, you will not be in the same place as someone else reading this book so it is impossible for me to tell you what to do next. Even if you have managed to implement some changes as you have gone along, you now potentially have a long list of actions in front of you that needs to be prioritised.

You need to decide which to do first, which to do last, which to do in between and in what sequence. That sounds simple, but it isn't. This is where all your hard work can potentially fall apart. Too much too soon is something you need to avoid. It is the temptation of most to treat every action as a priority. When it comes to strategy implementation, the early years after writing the corporate property strategy can often become overburdened with actions. If that is necessary, and you are able to allocate increased resources to do it, then great, but extra resources are unlikely. And remember, on the back of the corporate property strategy you have yet to pull together your asset management plan to pick up all the things you need to do with the property portfolio to deliver this strategy.

You can do it, but you need to pace yourself with the actions identified working through the 6 Ps methodology. Avoid being too ambitious too soon. Spread out the tasks. Hopefully there will be a prioritisation that has emerged naturally during the process. That may not always be so, in which case you will need to prioritise those tasks and secure a consensus to that prioritisation.

Check your bearings

There is a rule of thumb that aeroplane pilots often use to correct their navigation. It is called the 'One in sixty rule', and it goes like this: if the plane sets off on an incorrect course of just 1 degree, after 60 miles of flying, the plane will be 1 mile away from where it should be. That means if someone sets off to fly the 24,901-mile length of the Equator, the 1-degree error in direction at the start of the flight would see them over 400 miles away from where they should have been at the end of the flight. That's the equivalent of landing in Plymouth instead of Edinburgh. Lots of things can cause a plane to not keep to the original flight plan. That's why pilots will be regularly checking their bearings and airspeed. You have to do the same with your corporate property strategy. You cannot write the strategy and then sit back to leave it on autopilot. Things change and adjustments need to be made. No strategy should be so fixed it is incapable of flexibility to adapt to changing circumstances or priorities. Whichever board or other internal body has had oversight of the drafting process should regularly be taking stock of progress being made and changes to previous plans that might be necessary. This is essential.

Corporate property strategy structure

What the 6 Ps process gives you is not only a methodology that breaks things down into manageable pieces. It also provides, if you choose to use it this way, a structure for the strategy itself. Not everyone will want to use the 6 Ps that way, but if you have never created a corporate property strategy before, then it is not a bad place to start with your drafting, even if you depart from it as the drafting evolves.

If you decide to structure your corporate property strategy around the 6 Ps, here is what it might look like. You will notice the structure does not explicitly refer to the 6 Ps at all, but the content within each of the six sections can follow the 6 Ps in sequence:

- The property estate (Portfolio)
- What property assets do we own?
- What are the main segments?
- Our vision (Purpose)
- Why do we have property assets?
- What is each segment for?
- How we are doing (Performance)
- What are our aspirations for the property portfolio?
- How close are we to achieving those aspirations?

- Future management (Policies)
- How do we expect the property portfolio to be managed?
- What new (or different) rules do we need in place?
- Resources (People)
- What is the best model to deliver our aspirations and achieve our vision?
- What capabilities and resources will be needed?
- Governance (Process)
- How should strategic decisions be taken?
- What operational arrangements need to change?

By following a structured methodology, you will have realised that your corporate property strategy is likely to be as much about what you do not have in place, as what you do have in place. You will also appreciate how one element influences the next and their interlocking importance. Following this step-by-step process will have brought you clarity you may not have had before.

Summary

Creation of a property strategy is not an easy task; it takes a great deal of work and preparation. My hope is that, with this book and the 6 Ps methodology by your side, your task will be made easier. You will not be uncertain of what shape your strategy should take, what to include and exclude, and who to involve and who not to involve in the process. Instead, you have a tried-and-tested methodology to follow, fashioned out of over four decades of experience.

Conclusion

You have now seen what the 6 Ps are all about, and how they all link together. You have seen how understanding the purpose of your property portfolio is challenging without first having a clear and deep understanding of the portfolio and the segments within it. You have also learned it will be difficult to deliver on the purpose for your property portfolio unless you have a performance management framework in place. These are the three 'push' elements of the 6 Ps methodology. You then progressed into the three 'pull' elements of the 6 Ps methodology, realising the importance of having a clear policy framework, clarity on the people you need to deliver the organisational strategy and the role of clear operational and strategic processes. By working through the 6 Ps methodology I have mapped out for you, you will know where you are currently, and where you want to be.

Portfolio: You are clear on what your property portfolio is all about, what it contains and the main portfolio segments. If not, then you have a plan of action to do more work in this area. That might mean more detailed analysis or segmentation. It might have triggered thoughts of a rationalisation of the property portfolio, which you will need to revisit.

Purpose: You have established, or started to establish, enough clear purpose for your property portfolio to give your first corporate property strategy some real direction and clarity.

Performance: You have established what you do and don't know about the performance of your property portfolio. You have a plan to fill the gaps in your performance knowledge. Not only that, but your performance framework is also now clearly linked to your portfolio purpose, rather than being a ragbag of performance measures with no clear structure.

Policies: You now have a clear idea what property policies you need to have in place for your portfolio purpose to be implemented. My guess is that this is a daunting list, but you have achieved a great deal more than many do.

People: Now you know what your portfolio is, what its purpose is, how you want it to perform, and the policy framework necessary to reach your destination, you have been able to articulate what people resources are needed to achieve your goals. 'How many of what type' of roles, the skills you need, and as important, how these resources need to be structured. Don't underestimate what you have achieved if you have done that. Most staffing structures are either built on what people already have or an untested ideology as to what it should be.

Process: And finally, to the process element of the 6 Ps. You have built a comprehensive structure of both operational and governance processes you will need to serve the organisation and the corporate property strategy well. People will be clear on who does what, who decides what and what factors are taken into account in making those decisions. Believe me, not many organisations can say that with confidence.

The 6 Ps in practice

Does the 6 Ps methodology work in practice? I am going to share a story with you. One of my clients appointed me to advise whether their property team was fit for purpose given the size of their commercial property portfolio and the council's organisational objectives.

One challenge with this brief is there had, in the past, been no specific work done on determining whether or not, and how, the property portfolio was intended to support organisational objectives. Without knowing that, it would be tricky to know how the commercial portfolio needed to be managed to achieve those objectives and what size and make-up of property team would be needed.

Many reading this might think that the portfolio segmentation had already been done for me. After all, I was being asked to review the day-to-day management and delivery aspect of a specific part of the council's estate. But this is where portfolio segmentation gets interesting. Nobody should assume segmentation undertaken in the past is reliable. Unless there is a clear and recent audit trail showing how segmentation was done, who did it, the governance arrangements around it and a clear rationale for the segments, your first response should be to approach any previous segmentation with caution.

That was the case here. On the face of it, the segmentation had been done. Only it hadn't. The commercial portfolio needed further segmentation, driven by a clear purpose (see Chapter 4). Nobody really knew how properties had ended up in the council's commercial portfolio. There was some suggestion it was almost a default position, with everything that was not operational ending up there. Some of the portfolio was clearly more 'commercial' than others. There

CONCLUSION

had not been any recent discussion about why the portfolio was held. Some assets were more akin to investment properties (although not necessarily all classified as such in the balance sheet), some were out of centre retail properties that supported access to neighbourhood shopping, some were retail properties beneath residential tower blocks nobody knew what to do with and some properties were leased to local charities (and not on commercial terms).

When I started a dialogue with different stakeholders on the commercial portfolio, it was clear there were differences of opinion as to why the portfolio was held. Following a detailed analysis of the portfolio, we arrived at five distinct segments within the commercial portfolio: pure investments, low-cost business space, development opportunities, post-Covid support and recovery properties (obviously very time specific!) and voluntary and community properties. Through a disciplined approach we had moved from what, at the outset, was a single portfolio segment, to five distinct segments, each with its own characteristics and own purpose.

With that next level down of segmentation done, it was then possible to start to think what the different performance matrices (see Chapter 5) might be for each segment, what different property policies (see Chapter 6) might be necessary, what skills and capabilities might be needed to manage each segment (see Chapter 7) and what different work processes (see

Chapter 8) would be appropriate for each segment. This is a classic example of the power of the insight you might get working through the 6 Ps methodology.

Saying you need to take action now is an easy thing for me to say. Taking that action is another matter. Some may read this book and disagree with the methodology. That is their right, of course. Perhaps you feel you don't need a methodology or have a different one you follow. This methodology is built on experience and knowledge. Knowledge of what works and what doesn't. Observation over more than two decades of where things go wrong, and why they go wrong. All I seek to do is to prepare you based on my experience and insights. I hope these insights serve you as well as they have served me.

References

1. National Audit Office, 'Financial Sustainability of Local Authorities Visualisation: Update' (NAO, 2021)
2. Office for National Statistics, 'UK National Accounts: Blue Book 2021' (released October 2021). All data is available under the Open Government Licence v3.0.
3. B Thompson, 'Strategic public sector property asset management, Global 3rd edition' (Royal Institution of Chartered Surveyors, 2021)
4. Ibid
5. J Berman, 'The IKEA Effect: Study finds consumers over-value products they build themselves', *Huffpost* (September 2011), www.huffingtonpost.co.uk/entry/ikea-effect-consumers-study_n_981918, accessed 28 July 2022
6. Isaac Newton, *Philosophiæ Naturalis Principia Mathematica* (Royal Society & Edmund Halley, 1687)
7. J Read Hawthorne, *Diamonds, Pearls & Stones: Jewels of wisdom for young women from extraordinary women of the world* (Health Communications Inc, 2004)

8. 'How to Develop a Logic Model', Compass (no date), https://thecompassforsbc.org/how-to-guides/how-develop-logic-model-0, accessed 25 July 2022
9. 'Word: Shoshin', Kinfolk (no date), www.kinfolk.com/word-shoshin, accessed 25 July 2022
10. A C Doyle, *A Scandal in Bohemia* (Longman, 1999)
11. International Building Operation Standard, RICS (2021)
12. H Siebert, *Der Kobra-Effekt. Wie man Irrwege der Wirtschaftspolitik vermeidet* [in German] (Deutsche Verlags-Anstalt, 2001)
13. B Thompson, 'Strategic public sector property asset management, Global 3rd edition' (Royal Institution of Chartered Surveyors, 2021)
14. 'Asset Management: Overview, principles and terminology', British Standard ISO 55000 Series Kit (British Standards Institution, 2018)
15. S Heidari-Robinson, *Reorg: How to get it right* (Harvard Business Review Press, 2016)
16. Ibid
17. C Northcote Parkinson, *Parkinson's Law: Or the Pursuit of Progress* (1st Readers Union/John Murray, 1957)
18. Guide to developing the project business case (Crown copyright 2018)

Acknowledgements

This book is the culmination of over forty years in the local government sector. In that time, I have worked alongside some truly great people, each of them providing inspiration, support, guidance and motivation. There are simply too many to mention all by name, but there are three people that warrant a special mention.

The first is Robert (Bob) Morrissey, my first manager when I joined local government straight from school. He encouraged my interest in all things property, provided development support and gave me freedom to think and act.

Second, Bob Whyatt, who was City Valuer at Bristol City Council during my time there. He supported me through my professional qualification, saw the 'strategic' in me and blessed me with several promotions.

Thirdly, my CIPFA colleague, Susan Robinson, who always inspired me to be the best I could be in my consultancy and training work by setting and demanding the highest possible standards in everything.

I must thank my advance readers. I can't thank them enough for taking the time to give me such helpful and constructive feedback. This book is so much better for their input. Thank you, Tony Bamford, Jonathan Fearn, Susan Robinson, Sophie Linton, Paul Kettrick and Gary Woodhouse.

During the preparation for this book, I was very grateful to a number of people that gave up their valuable time to contribute to my research. Thank you, Allan Harty, Edward Jones, Ross McLaughlin, Gillian Blackford, Daniella Barrow, Rebecca Couch, Emily White, Jonathan Fearn, Fay Hayward, Paul Jones, Sue Harries, Mike Harries, Ian Turner, Dan Bates, Councillor Keith House, Jonny Alford, Tony Bamford, Stuart Knight, Abigail Marshall, Laura Stamboulieh, David Harris, Rob Tozer, Rob Huntington, Colin Lewington, Joanne Jones, David Pethen and Arthur Pritchard.

Writing this book has been fun and exhausting. But most of all I have found it uplifting. I have thoroughly enjoyed the process of releasing experiences hidden

ACKNOWLEDGEMENTS

away in the depths of my memory, so that I can share them with you.

I would like to thank the team at Rethink Press, who inspired me to get my experiences down on paper and motivated me through the writing process. Thank you, Lucy McCarraher, Joe Gregory, Roger Waltham, Anke Ueberberg, Kate Latham and Lisa Cooper.

To start writing a book needs a spark. It needs someone to plant the idea in your head that writing a book and sharing years of insights would be a good idea, and to give you confidence that people will want to read it. For me, that person was Daniel Priestley of Dent Global. Thank you, Dan, for helping me see my 'mountain of value'.

Finally, thank you to my patient wife Sue, for putting up with me constantly talking about the book and providing updates on the writing process, but supporting me for months on end all the way.

The Author

Chris is a highly experienced property asset manager, consultant, trainer and speaker. He has reached a stage in his forty-year distinguished career in the public sector where the most important thing for him is leaving a legacy through knowledge sharing. He is a leading advocate and influencer for strategic asset management in the public sector, with first-hand practical skills in developing asset strategies and implementing change for clients across the UK.

Over the past twenty years, Chris has worked in a consultancy capacity with some of the largest local authorities in the UK. Chris is a knowledgeable and practical management consultant, skilled in diagnosing strategic asset management problems and devising tailored solutions for his clients.

It has been calculated the combined balance sheet value of the consultancy clients Chris has worked with exceeds £60 billion. He has trained over 15,000 people and is well-known and respected across the sector for his knowledge and experience. Through social media, Chris is known for drawing upon analogies and experiences outside of the public sector and outside of the property industry, finding ways to communicate complex concepts in an easy-to-understand manner and with his unique insights.

Chris is passionate about sport, enjoys playing badminton and – for his sins – is a season ticket holder at Bristol City FC. Chris is also a musician, having learned the trombone at age seven, going on to play in both the City of Bristol and County of Avon orchestras. When time allows, he is also an amateur genealogist and has been researching his family tree for a number of years. A keen nature lover, Chris describes himself as a 'birder' (as opposed to 'twitcher') and he also dabbles in photography.

- www.chrisbrainassociates.com
- www.linkedin.com/in/chris-brain-a0035918
- www.facebook.com/ChrisBrainAssociates

Printed in Great Britain
by Amazon